The

RPG World Book

BY ELMORE

A Comic Quest for Wealth, Power, and all that Other Good Stuff...

*

www.larryelmore.com

The SnarfQuest™ RPG World Book

Conceptualization and Original SnarfQuest Comic:	Larry Elmore
Writing & Design:	Jamie Chambers
Additional Writing & Design:	Larry Elmore, Ken Whitman, Trevis Powell, Jim Wardrip, and Tony Lee
Cover and Interior Art:	Larry Elmore
Project Management:	Ken Whitman
Editing:	Tony Lee
Proofreading:	Trevis Powell, Christopher Coyle, Renae Chambers, Lester Smith, and Tony Lee

Dedication:

SnarfQuest is about a journey with friends, full of humor and adventure. For that reason, I'd like to dedicate this to my friends Ken Whitman, Tony Lee, and Don Perrin for being part of my own quest since the beginning. It's been a blast!

—Jamie Chambers

Published by

Elmore Productions, Inc.
P.O. Box 358
Leitchfield, KY 42755
www.larryelmore.com

ISBN 0-9722468-6-X
Printed in the United States

A Word from Larry Elmore about SnarfQuest™ RPG World Book

First of all, I want to thank all the people out there that have read and supported The SnarfQuest comic strip. From talking to a great number of you, over the years, I truly feel that you have enjoyed reading it as much as I have writing and illustrating it. For all of you that have wanted to take the next step and join that wacky world of Snarf, here is your chance.

Each year I attend several fantasy and science fiction conventions and I always get a kick when people discover that I am the dude who does Snarf. They have a hard time separating the "serious" painter from the silly dude that creates that stupid comic strip!! Also at these conventions, many people relive, with me, their favorite Snarf episode. Some people have told me how much pleasure the SnarfQuest graphic novel brought them while sitting in the desert during Desert Storm. Not only American troops have told me this but other soldiers from other countries. They tell me how their company or battalion had only one old worn copy that was passed around and treated with reverence. It pleases me that I can make someone smile and that my humor crosses many boundaries. You don't have to be a fantasy freak to enjoy Snarf.

In this book, I tell you a lot of my thoughts behind the adventures of Snarf, and some of the characters. The main thing this game book tries to do is help show you ways to add some humor in your gaming. I think we succeeded in many ways.

Many people tell me how long it had been since they laughed out loud by simply reading a comic strip and they want to know how I came up with so many humorous situations. The truth is that the basic premise of the strip (seeking adventures) comes from my childhood. Some of my cousins, friends and I were always roaming the woods seeking an adventure. We succeeded in having a few and occasionally scaring the crap out of ourselves. I was very fortunate to grow up in a rural where there was no TV's, or video games at the time (I was VERY young then---I am really telling my age now). People had to entertain themselves and they were not dependent on a machine for 95% of their entertainment. One form of entertainment was telling stories; funny or scary stories were the most popular. It was a slower paced life then and I had the time and opportunity to meet some real characters, and I will admit that some of these people were my relatives. Even though we were poor and had a lot of hardships, we laughed a lot and it seemed that almost everyone I knew had a wild sense of humor.

ELMORE

Table of Contents

The (MIS)Adventure Begins...

And so, with the passing of Zingart the Sneak, king of the valley (which occurred in a most embarrassing way), the tribe again entered in to the dangerous year of succession. For one year, the council of elders ruled the valley while the bravest warriors ventured into the greater world. For those who remained in the valley, there would be uncertainty. For those who quested for the throne, there would be dangers and wonders.

Over a half-dozen zeetvahs left the valley in search of treasure and fame. Two came home within a week (one crying). One candidate was reportedly chased off the Cliffs of Evritt by a lasher-beast. Three wandered far off to the west, where rumors say one settled down with an attractive elf-maiden of dubious reputation. The remaining two warriors returned with legitimate claims to the throne.

The first warrior to return home was Newfert ben'Dares (the bold). The final young warrior to return was the most unlikely of them all, yet he was destined to be our people's greatest king. His name was Snarfenja de'Gottago—known by one and all simply as "Snarf."

—The Chronicles of *Nolmer the Scribe*,
History of the Throne, Eighth Month, Year of the Frog

INTRODUCTION

Welcome to the world of SnarfQuest! Here you may encounter adventuring zeetvahs, cross paths with time-traveling mages, assist stranded robots, and meet dozens of beautiful women. Journey in a land where Lady Luck changes the fortunes of the foolish and the brave. Recover treasure from a dragon's lair or a warlock's keep. Grab your bedroll and wineskin, strap on your backpack and boots, sharpen your sword and shine your helmet. The road calls, and adventure awaits!

HISTORY OF SNARFQUEST

SnarfQuest began in 1983 as a black-and-white comic strip drawn by Larry Elmore, the fantasy artist largely responsible for re-defining the "look" of fantasy role-playing games in the early 80's. *Dragon Magazine* was the home of three pages of SnarfQuest until 1989, when Elmore retired the strip to concentrate on freelance work. Always one of the most popular features of the magazine, fans wrote in for years hoping for more Snarf.

With the launch of *Games Unplugged* magazine, fans got their wish. Now SnarfQuest is back every other month—this time in full color! Now the world of SnarfQuest is opened up for gamers everywhere using the d20 System, fully compatible with the Third Edition of the most popular role-playing game in the world.

I see the earth during the time of Snarf as a very ancient time, long before recorded history. Perhaps in an antediluvian world. There are plenty of ancient races during this time. Snarf is a Zeetvah, which is one of those races. These ancients, to me, are Mother Nature's attempts to evolve intelligent mammals and, for some reason or another, they didn't make it and eventually became extinct. In my mind, these races were old by the time dwarves and elves were established in fantasy lore. In this period, humans are the most recent race on earth and are quickly populating more and more territories. This is a time that any type of race could exist and one race would not be surprised by the looks or quirks of another. This gives me total freedom to draw any kind of intelligent or semi-intelligent critter that pops into my head. With this creative freedom, Snarf could go over a hill or beyond a mountain and run into anything you would like to dream up.

THE D20 SYSTEM

This product uses the d20 System and requires the use of the Dungeons & Dragons Player's Handbook, Third Edition, published by Wizards of the Coast. The game material presented in this book does not stand alone, and assumes ownership of core d20 System products.

The SnarfQuest campaign setting has unique features, which differ from core d20 System products. These features are designed to bring to life the fantasy world of Larry Elmore's SnarfQuest. Whenever material in this book contradicts something from another product (including races, classes, skills, feats, and magic), your game will be enhanced if this book takes precedence.

Or, as Snarf would say: "Dees rules will make da game more fun!"

OVERVIEW OF SNARF'S WORLD

Snarf begins his quest knowing next to nothing about the outside world, and even in his extensive travels only covers a small part of a large continent. Full knowledge of the world (or even a complete map!) is still many centuries away.

This is a young world, largely uncivilized. Vast tracts of untamed wilderness lie between isolated communities and small city-states. Humans are only one race among dozens, and hold no greater power than elves, zeetvahs, or almeers. Powerful wizards pursue magical research in remote towers while druids gain power in hidden stone circles. Wild animals and savage monsters own the wilderness, which is crossed only in large groups or by brave (and not-so-brave) adventurers.

ADVENTURING, SNARFQUEST STYLE

The basic elements of a SnarfQuest campaign are much like typical fantasy adventures. It is, after all, the pursuit of wealth, power, and all that other good stuff! With just a few additions and a slight change in tone, any game can have the right attitude to reflect the exploits of Larry Elmore's zany zeetvah.

Snarf's world is one where there are just as many "critter" races of anthropomorphic humanoids as there are humans, elves, and the like. It's a place in which wizards time-travel to gain knowledge of advanced technology (or occasionally motorcycles and light beer). It's a place where every lady is beautiful, every quest takes strange turns, and heroes come in all sizes.

Even without the specifics of Snarf's world, this book can be used as a way to introduce more humor into a fantasy d20 System campaign. A light-hearted adventure or silly quest provides a nice break from the usual gritty storylines, and make serious, epic plots seem more important by breaking the dramatic tension with the occasional comedy episode.

So grab your dice, your buddies, and a gaming table. There are good times ahead!

Ye Old Young Lands

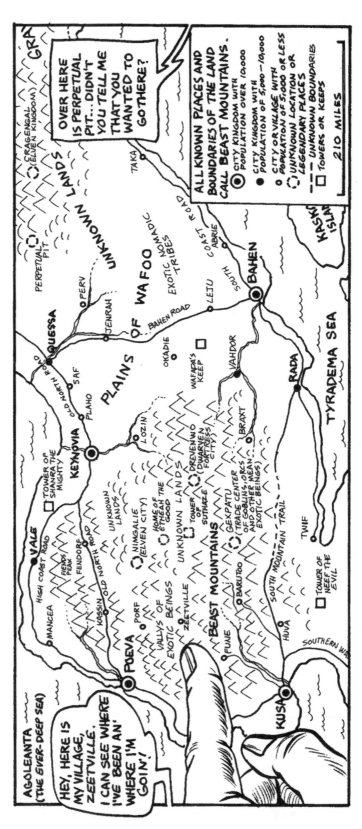

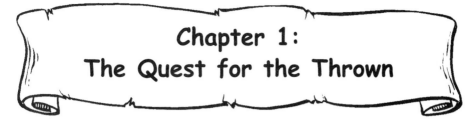

Chapter 1:
The Quest for the Thrown

The chronicles of Snarf's quest for the throne of the valley is required reading for young zeetvahs. Written by Nolmer, royal scribe, they tell the triumphs, tragedies, fortunes, and follies that led to Snarf becoming the king of all zeetvahs. Snarf's story (as seen in the SnarfQuest comic strip) is also chock full of great ideas that can be used for adventures in Snarf's world or humorous gaming in general.

The whole concept of the SnarfQuest adventure was just like a role playing game. I had a very simple quest, and that was it. Once the quest for king was established, I had no preconceived details of the story. I just wanted it to be a great adventure. When I started writing each episode, I never knew what would happen next. Usually I never thought about the story until I started doing the next episode. It was all totally spontaneous. It constantly got easier as the characters developed; eventually the characters seem to write their own story.

EPISODE #1: "A QUEST LAUNCHED" (or "A Lesson in Hospitality")

The story of Snarf begins with the senile zeetvah elder reminding everyone of the recent death of the king (who died in a most embarrassing way). Zeetvahs have ruled the valley because of their great leadership, which in turn is a measure of how they choose their leaders. A one-year quest is set for all zeetvah warriors: "Ze warrior zat has acquired ze most riches or performed ze most heroic deeds" will be the next king. Snarf, a young zeetvah of humble origins, decided he could exchange one year of hard work for a lifetime on "easy street" as king. With only his sword and raw courage, he set out to prove himself. For weeks, he walked, ate, and slept without a single hint of danger or adventure.

Roasting a strange bird on his fire, Snarf pondered his terrible fortune when a burly orc wandered into the camp.

"Would ya share yer fire and a bite to eat?" asked the lonely orc. Snarf agreed, first startled by the orc's sudden appearance, and then intrigued by the large jewel in the orc's horned helm. His first plan was to knock the orc unconscious, but when that idea failed Snarf resorts to prying the jewel out with his sword while the orc slept. The orc woke up with the zeetvah's blade-tip in his face and stumbled backwards, tripping and losing his helmet in the process. Snarf took advantage of the situation and chased after the orc, hollering that he was a "mad, crazed, buzzerker." Once the orc was several leagues away, Snarf took the jewel and continued his quest, happy to accumulate his first piece of treasure.

I first created the premise to launch the SnarfQuest adventure, which was a little silly, but as I started writing and illustrating the story, I had a problem as soon as Snarf left his village. I had to introduce some element that was funny and get Snarf off to a good start. I thought of an orc coming into Snarf's camp and at first I had the orc attacking Snarf. That would be the normal thing everyone would think of. So I reversed it. I had a nice ol' orc and Snarf ends up attacking him. I found that if I took a normal event and gave it a twist it would add constant flavor to the story. Never a dull moment!

Adventure Notes

Story Arcs: Individual adventures are great, but episodic stories (such as television, comic books, and role-playing games) are often more exciting with longer, continuous story arcs. Although Snarf will have many independent adventures ahead, they are all part of his own quest to become king.

Let the Players Take Initiative: Most adventure games have the referee take the lead in moving the plot along. But in humor games, it's better to introduce a simple, non-threatening premise and let the players decide what to do with it. The orc presented no danger to Snarf, merely wanting his company and a bite to eat, but the sight of the gem enticed our hero's greed.

Run With Strange Ideas: If this episode had been a gaming session, the orc might have been included for a completely different reason. Perhaps he had a clue to Snarf's next adventure, or was a possible addition to the party. But when Snarf-as-player-character decided to rob the orc and start chasing him off, it served the story to go with the flow rather than fighting it. Humorous gaming is about spontaneity and letting the players shape each encounter, with a fast-thinking referee to improvise.

EPISODE #2: PRINCE RAT...ER, RAFFENDORF

Snarf continued along the forest trail when he witnessed a strange sight, a man-sized giant rat with huge round ears, a sword, armor, and an eyepatch. The overgrown rodent just stood there with his foot stuck in the ground. The "rat" claimed to be a human prince named Raffendorf, cursed to wear the form of a rat until he could find someone to restore

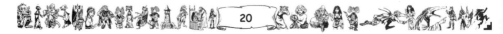

his true body. Raffendorf also told Snarf that a nasty little beast had grabbed and trapped his foot in its den.

Snarf attempted to stab the critter following Raffendorf's directions, but it only got angrier—taking the rat-man's boot off and biting down on his toes. Snarf, swinging his sword in reverse like a club, knocked the creature over the center-field bleachers.

Raffendorf was quite grateful for Snarf's aid, but when Snarf demanded money the prince claimed to be "a little low on cash at the moment," but insisted that he knew of a place in which great wealth could be found. Snarf was skeptical, but still opts to travel with Raffendorf.

Adventure Notes

Introduce New Characters: Most role-playing campaigns just have everyone starting out at the same time. While you don't want to bore the other players, it's more interesting to introduce characters one at a time. This lets everyone be "in the spotlight" when they debut, and gives the whole group a better idea of who they are.

Monsters Don't Always Attack: Mix things up for encounters with monsters, like biting and dragging a character's foot down a hole. Some problems can't be solved with mindless violence. They require strategy, clever thinking, or even luck.

I would hardly ever introduce new characters in a normal way, like shaking hands and introducing yourself. I would always try to create an event, and the event was usually funny. This would move the story and add to the whole comedic effect. The first character that would travel with Snarf was Raffendorf, and he had troubles and issues of his own. Raffendorf's problems led them on their first quest. The SnarfQuest comic strip was never planned very much, especially at first. It was very spontaneous, just like a role-playing game. I had no clue, when I started writing each episode, what would happen next. If something was interesting or funny, I just went with it.

EPISODE #3: THE EVIL RIDER

Snarf and Raffendorf prepared to make camp in a clearing, with Snarf making the fire and Raf out finding a meal. Suddenly a bearded evil rider charged in on a white horse, testing his axemanship on poor Snarf. The zeetvah bravely fled for his life. Finding a knee-deep pond, he ducked underwater, using a hollow reed to breathe.

Meanwhile, a bombardier bee (unique to SnarfQuest, of course) flew his way across the pond. Its wings were tired, and the bug decided to rest right on the very reed Snarf was using to breathe! Snarf blew the bee clear up into the air with one big breath. The bug was convinced it had been killed by a "bug-eatin' weed" and was on its way to Bug Heaven. When it began to fall, it was sure it was doomed to Bug Hell, and that the dark rider was a demon! With a kamikaze scream, the bug dove for the dark rider's helmet…

Adventure Notes

Never An Ordinary Day: Things never stay normal in the world of SnarfQuest. Even something as mundane as building a campfire soon became a dangerous battle! If things begin to calm down for too long during a game, throw in a random, bizarre peril and make the players think fast.

Strange Turns of Luck: The good fortune of heroes sometimes has no direct correlation to them or their actions! It can manifest itself in strange ways, with the most comical results. Snarf never knew the role the bee played in saving his life, though the rest of us certainly do. Use these asides in the game as well.

EPISODE #4: HOWLS IN THE NIGHT (or Much Ado About Nothing)

The bombardier bee shot into the black rider's helmet—determined to "sting his face off." Snarf heard the rider's screams even from underwater. He looked up to see the poor evil warrior running around, trying to pry off his helm. Snarf took immediate advantage of the situation, clonking the warrior on the head with his trusty sword. The dark rider collapsed like a sack of flour, with the bee staggering away, glad that it had been "weinca'nated."

Raffendorf returned, having heard the dark rider's screams, and found Snarf calmly looting the unconscious knight. Raffendorf found it hard to believe that Snarf had fought the warrior alone, but was impressed nonetheless.

Later, in the dark of the night, the duo pressed on—wishing to put some distance between themselves and the probably-vengeful warrior. Treading cautiously, a horrifying wail pierced the darkness. Snarf and Raf, afflicted with pants-wetting fear, were convinced it was "some kind of monster" and the two beat feet to flee whatever made the sound. Running at night is unsafe* and the two tumbled down a hill like Jack and Jill. All was quiet, and the heroic pair thought they had escaped, when suddenly the wail broke out again—right in front of them! A quick glance revealed the "monster" was but a tiny lizard, which made a disgustingly squishy sound under the pair's flat blades.

Don't try this at home, kids!

Adventure Notes

Heroes Are Made, Not Born: Snarf may not have realized the dark rider was being stung in the face by a bee, but he knew perfectly well that something weird was going on, yet he was perfectly content to let Raffendorf think he bested the rider in single combat. Exaggerations about such events are what the heroes of SnarfQuest are made of.

Don't Let 'Em Get Cocky: Just when Snarf was full of confidence, he let a tiny lizard scare the squittle-dee-do out of him. If the adventurers in your game start to think they are "all that," a little humiliation is just what they need to keep a proper SnarfQuest perspective.

EPISODE #5: BABE #1 (or A Powerful Sorceress In Distress)

Snarf was impatient for treasure and glory, hounding Raffendorf with the annoyance of a child stuck on a long car trip. The pair's argument was interrupted, however, by the sounds of a woman crying. Investigation led to a beautiful brunette sniffling and whimpering. Snarf, with all the charm he could muster, asked "What's yer problem, babe?" The occasionally-dynamic duo learned the woman was Etheah of the Woodland, a good sorceress who fought the evil wizard Suthaze with the help of a magical wishing wand—that is, until Suthaze stole it from her. Etheah offered the heroes a wish each if they could recover her wand, an offer they could not refuse, even though the name Suthaze made Raffendorf squirm.

A couple of nights later, in the Tower of Suthaze™, the apprentice Geezel watched the Magic Time-Jumping Glass for when his boss, the evil and mighty Suthaze, would return from a trip to the future. Suthaze did return, crashing a futuristic horse machine into the wall and leaking gasoline on the floor. Geezel contended that all of Suthaze's trips to the future were a waste of time, trading good jewels for "junk." Suthaze corrected the young apprentice by pulling out a revolver. "Listen moon mouth—this time I found the ultimate magic weapon…and I know how to use it."

Adventure Notes

Beautiful Women in Need: All women are beautiful in Larry Elmore's world (see Chapter Four: Humor), but the cream of the crop are in need of something: magic wands, rescuing from an evil wizard and his dragon, or help avenging her long-dead father (for easy-to-find examples). Lusty, egotistical SnarfQuest heroes are just the sort to jump at any quest given to them by such a damsel. (If you have female players in your group, use male equivalents.)

Yep, almost all women are beautiful in Snarf's world. I think it is because I love 'em and see beauty in most all women. Sometimes the most beautiful woman is the most dangerous. I guess, because I am a man, it is easier for me to tell what is inside a man's head. Therefore, I tend to exaggerate men more in their appearance, in order to illustrate their inner character. A woman, any woman, especially a beautiful woman, can get one over on me any time she wishes, I just can't help it. I guess I am just a sucker when it comes to women, and Snarf is for sure!!

Provide the Unexpected: Traditional fantasy wizards don't ride motorcycles or carry pistols, do they? In SnarfQuest, villains are just too weird to predict. If you want standard fare, you're running the wrong game world.

EPISODE #6: DON'T SHOOT AT YOUR BOSS

The argument between Geezel and Suthaze continued, the little ("nice") almeer fed up with the constant insults from the old wizard. Geezel ended up holding the pistol, and accidentally shot the Magic Time-Jumping Glass (only a Major Magical Artifact!) and almost hitting the wizard. Suthaze, of course, was calm in his response: "I'm gonna KILL YOU!!" followed by a lightning bolt. Geezel hiked up his robe and ran for his life.

Snarf and Raf, meanwhile, were able to enter the tower thanks to Snarf's lock-picking skills. They heard someone coming, and set up an ambush—for Geezel! Snarf seized the "magic weapon" (the revolver, remember?) and stashed it while Raf marveled over their luck at capturing Suthaze's apprentice. Geezel offered to team up with the pair, hoping they could help him survive Suthaze's wrath. In the interim, Suthaze watched the whole episode via his crystal ball.

EPISODE #7: THE TREASURY
(or "He Needs a Bigger Bowl")

At swordpoint, Geezel led Snarf and Raffendorf through a secret passage to the tower treasury. Snarf was the first to charge in, only to quickly charge back out again, scared out of his wits! He had seen a huge dragon in the treasury, and was ready to kill Geezel for not supplying that bit of information. Geezel was quick to explain that "Willie" was a dragon who had been enchanted to think he was a duck. As long as no one said the word "dragon" around him, the spell would maintain.

True to Geezel's word, the dragon did turn out to be a pathetic specimen, sitting in a bowl full of water and lisping his words.

Snarf and Raffendorf began collecting the wands, including a few that were souvenirs from Suthaze's time-jumps into the future.

As Snarf and Raf were busy looting, Suthaze gathered his minions to storm the treasury…

Adventure Notes
Appearances Can Be Deceiving: This would become a recurring theme, but was first made evident with Willie the dragon. Assumptions are often false in SnarfQuest, where misdirection is commonplace. Just when you are sure of something, the plot takes a left turn.

EPISODE #8: THE GREAT ESCAPE (or "Frying Bacon")
Snarf and Raf continued looting the treasury. Snarf discovered a "wand of light" (which looks suspiciously like a flashlight). He also loaded down his pouch with gold and jewels,

while Raf and Geezel begged him to leave. On the way out, Snarf came up with an inspired plan. He ran back into the treasury and shouted "Dragon—Dragon—Dragon" as loud as he could, breaking the spell over Willie. The trio made record time up the stairs while the newly awakened dragon roared in fury.

Suthaze and his guards were in hot pursuit, stopped only when "Willie" stuck his head out of the treasury door. Suthaze was confused, and the dragon was too happy to explain: "My name is Kizarvexius, and you are about to become bacon!" Suthaze magically teleported himself away, just before the dragon fried Suthaze's minions.

Snarf and company were leaving when a feminine voice called out for help behind a barred door. The zeetvah could not resist. He opened the door to a lovely young maiden in "light" costume. Snarf was convinced this was his lucky day!

Adventure Notes
Let Clever Plans Work: Although risky, it was clever of ol' Snarf to break the spell on Willie—and the gamble wiped out most of the opposition. When your players come up with really clever plans you hadn't anticipated, reward them with success. If zany, risky plans work for the group, they'll try them more often than resorting to the old standby of hackin' and spell slingin'.

EPISODE #9: MY HEROES

Snarf was quick to lay it on thick with the unnamed damsel, bragging about his exploits and his future plans. She seemed to hang on every word! Finding the front door unguarded, the group escaped from the tower. They were about to get away scot-free, but the maiden quickly ran out of breath.

After a quick rest, the woman shifted her attention from Snarf to Geezel, and gave the little almeer a big hug—suddenly POOFing to show that "she" was actually Suthaze in disguise! The group was quickly overwhelmed by Suthaze's superior magical powers, and Raffendorf finally confessed it was Suthaze who transformed him into a giant rat in the first place! The wizard remembered the prince as well, and decided to transform him yet again, this time into a strange little flying bug! Snarf realized the "magic weapon" (i.e., the revolver) might be their only hope, but also that he had no clue how to use it.

EPISODE #10: DESTRUCTION OF THE TOWER (or "Quack?!")

Snarf and Suthaze wrestled over the revolver, with Geezel shouting instructions to help the zeetvah. A shot rang out. The bullet sped through the window of Suthaze's tower, ricocheted past jars of highly explosive magical powder and finally hit the wooden table, knocking a lit candle off… which rolled right into the pool of gasoline left by the motorcycle—er, horse machine! The resulting explosion was spectacular, clearly seen and heard by Suthaze and our heroes.

As Suthaze looked at the smoking remains of his former lair, dumbfounded, Snarf stared in wonder at the revolver, convinced it was a weapon of unbelievable destruction. In the tower ruins, Kizarvexius the dragon staggered around, stupefied by the explosion. He only had one thing to say: "Quack?"

A ticked-off Suthaze prepared to cast a spell that would send the zeetvah to meet his maker (no, not Larry Elmore). Snarf closed his eyes and squeezed the trigger, shooting the evil wizard in the foot. The long-eared warrior could not bear to look, believing the shot would surely litter pieces of Suthaze all over the ground. Hearing the wizard's cries, he was disappointed to find that he had only blown a small hole in the old man's foot. Snarf and Raf beat a hasty retreat, with Geezel running fast behind.

Suthaze was able to recover shortly after, bandaging his foot and swearing revenge on the trio. The dragon staggered over to the wizard, asking: "Could you get me…quack…a bigger bowl to sthwim in?"

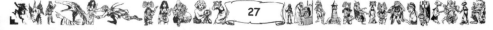

Adventure Notes

Unexpected Results: Just as clever plans should be rewarded, crazy things should happen completely out of the players' control. Snarf had no idea what he was doing, but managed to destroy the tower, boggle Suthaze, and render a dragon harmless with one misplaced aim.

Medieval Characters and Anachronisms: While Snarf has no clue what a pistol is, we the audience do, and we are highly amused by his assumption that every time he aims it at something there will be an awesome explosion. Players should role-play their characters with the appropriate knowledge, even when it means "playing dumb" and not taking every possible advantage. Reward players for doing it right—such as blowing up the evil wizard's tower.

EPISODE #11: JUST REWARDS
(or "Be Careful What You Wish For")

The party ran straight for Etheah's cottage. (Well, Raf was flying—he's a bug now, remember?) The sorceress (who apparently sleeps until noon) was courteous enough to swat the bug on his head. The eyepatched insect was in good enough shape to cuss about his mis-

fortune. Etheah perked up considerably to see her wand again. She granted a wish to each hero.

Raffendorf did not hesitate. "I wish to be back to my original self!" He was stunned when he was restored to rat-man form. Etheah (not the brightest of sorceresses) failed to see what he was fussing about.

Snarf watched Raffendorf completely lose his dignity, the former prince crying and banging his head up against a rock. "I wish you could see yourself!" Snarf chortled, going very wide-eyed when a mirror suddenly appeared in front of Raf. So much for Snarf's wish! Now it was Snarf's turn to whine, while Raf grinned with grim amusement.

Adventure Notes

Use Their Own Words Against Them: In a more serious game, players should be allowed careful planning and considered declaration of their actions. In a humorous setting, such as SnarfQuest, everything the players say can and should be used against them. If a player states something, assume his character is saying it, thinking it, or doing it. Keep them flustered, and they will supply plenty of amusing situations.

EPISODE #12: GEEZEL'S ENGAGEMENT

Snarf and Raf, frustrated they blew their own wish, were surprised when Etheah chose to grant Geezel a wish for helping find her wand. Both of them, of course, had "suggestions"

for what Geez should wish for. The almeer wisely ignored the arguing pair. His wish? "I wish dat Etheah fell in love wif me so much dat she wants me to stay here wif her to study magic so dat I may become a good powerful wizard!"

Sure enough, Etheah fell madly in love with Geezel and promptly proposed to him. Snarf interrupted, disgusted by the display. He showed Etheah the revolver. The horrified sorceress told Snarf that the weapon was a thing of evil and must be flung into the Perpetual Pit. She promised to reward him with a valuable gift if he promised to complete the task.

Raffendorf, meanwhile, seems to have had enough of quests. He volunteered to work for Etheah for a year, doing menial chores (especially for a prince) in order to get another shot at a wish.

EPISODE #13: ENTER THE ROBOT

While Geezel and Raffendorf argued over who was the smartest, Etheah revealed the "valuable gift" to Snarf: a magical pack of holding! Now Snarf could carry a ridiculous amount of equipment and treasure without weighing himself down. Impressed, he said his goodbyes and hit the trail, making his way toward the Perpetual Pit.

A month passed uneventfully as Snarf slogged along on foot. When he heard a strange noise in the sky, he looked up to see a "silver dragon" (though it looks suspiciously like a space ship) making a power dive toward the ground. The beast crashed, and Snarf ventured closer to investigate.

Emerging from the wreck was a short, fully armored warrior (though he looks suspiciously like a robot). Snarf dragged the little guy away, and after a few failed attempts to communicate the armored figure finally uttered a few words that Snarf could understand. When Snarf tried to explain what happened, the little guy was dismayed: "I am one stranded robot!"

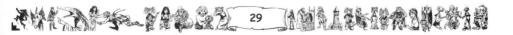

LATER.

SSSKKKEEEEIIIIOOOOoOUUUU......... KA-BLOW!!

?

WHAT IN DA WORLD?..

IT'S A SILVER DRAGON!

GAAAA!

Adventure Notes

Give 'Em Cool Stuff: Recovering Etheah's wand was a major quest, and while he blew his wish, he deserved something. Snarf could not have hauled his treasure around without the pack, and it became an important part of his adventuring.

Use Anachronisms: Snarf just keeps running into things that are out of place in his world: guns, flashlights, and now a robot! This is the zany trademark of SnarfQuest. Make full use of it in your own adventures. How medieval heroes interact with cars, radios, and Post-It notes can make for entertaining vignettes.

I must mention how Aveeare and Effim got their names. When I was in the Army, I was in a Combat Engineer battalion. I drove an armored track vehicle, an M577 command track. It was full of radios, and when we went on alerts, everyone in the track was talking on all these different radios. It seemed chaotic, but all I had to do was just drive the thing and keep up on all the maintenance. All of the radios had a letter prefix, usually VR or FM, then followed by a long number code. I just made my two robots in the comic strip the VR's and FM's of the future!

EPISODE #14: AVEEARE

The armored little warrior was lamenting the loss of his "ship." He and Snarf also had trouble communicating. Snarf was able to get the little guy's name, however. "I am a VR-X9 4 M2 Galactic Probe, Government Issue Robot." All Snarf could understand was "Aveeare," so it stuck.

An explosion interrupted their conversation, each convinced the other was either stupid or insane. Aveeare told Snarf it was his ship's power unit overloading, though Snarf was sure it was the dragon's last, big breath.

Aveeare told Snarf he would follow someone of importance so he could record this person's deeds. Snarf thought the revolver would impress the robot, so he went digging around inside the backpack. When Aveeare saw that Snarf was able to climb in to what appeared to be a small pack, Aveeare made a declaration: "You have proven to me that you can go beyond physical logic and the natural laws, I am at your service, sir!"

EPISODE #15:
FIGHTIN' AND SELF-PROTECTION

Snarf was pleased to have acquired a new companion (even if he could not understand half of the words Aveeare said). Snarf laid it on thick, asking for Aveeare to defend him while he was "meditating real deep about great things." Soon enough, the pair run into their first trouble, when a bandit leaped out of the trees on the North Road.

Aveeare was slow to realize they were in danger, but his blasters made short work of two bandits. Snarf was pleased, making a quick demand: "Give me all yer loot an' den you two split!" Aveeare did not even accept a share of the loot, saying he did not need money or treasures. The pair prepared to hit the road once more, when a goofy-looking figure emerged from the woods, asking for directions.

Adventure Notes

Let Them Cream Lesser Enemies: Heroes are supposed to fight ordinary foes and beat the stuffing out of them. Mere bandits were no match for Snarf and (especially) Aveeare. It's good to toss in an occasional throwaway encounter whose sole purpose is to showcase the characters.

EPISODE #16: ARRIVAL IN KEYNOVIA (or "Sgt. Dorque")

The newcomer introduced himself as "Dorque da Wanderer," and Snarf did his best to get rid of the bulbous-nosed buffoon. Dorque followed the zeetvah and robot, telling them: "I follow you 'cause you is goin' someplace." Aveeare suggested that Snarf hire Dorque to give them a scout and peace at the same time.

Dorque returned early the next morning, reporting that they were near a city called Keynovia. Snarf had never been to a human city before, and began throwing his money around, getting roaring drunk, buying expensive clothes and trinkets with his accumulated wealth. They soon needed a cart or wagon. Snarf drunkenly staggered over to Gabul's New & Used Transportation. "We want some wheelzz, somethin' fast an' (hic) cheap."

Adventure Notes

Encourage Excess: SnarfQuest is the quest for wealth, power, and all that other good stuff. The heroes shouldn't hoard their gold and spend it only on adventuring supplies. They want to live the good life, with fine clothes, great beer, and anything else they can afford. The characters should live it up, though they can certainly party too hard and get into trouble…

EPISODE #17: THE GAGGLEZOOMER

Gabul had just the thing for Snarf—a rare, bizarre reptile known as a gagglezoomer, a beast that would run incredibly fast when something touched it's sensitive back, then stop dead in its track when the offending object was removed. Despite Aveeare's warnings, Snarf purchased the 'zoomer and loaded up the cart.

The salesman showed Snarf the use of a "gagglestick" and a stranger creature he called a "gaggaleech," one obviously far too intelligent for such menial work. With drunken confidence, Snarf climbed into the driver's seat and they took off—immediately losing control of the gagglezoomer!

The 'zoomer cart flew through Kenovia at high speed, with Snarf valiantly trying to steer it. After bouncing off a few walls, Aveeare urged Snarf to stop the creature by removing the leech. Snarf leaned forward, trying to get the stick close enough for the leech to grab on…

Adventure Notes
Quick Changes of Pace: Snarf & Co. went from a drunken, leisurely trip to a local merchant to a life-threatening ride through a city lined with stone walls. Keep the players on their toes by suddenly shifting a slow encounter into a hair-raising gear!

Luck, good or bad, is a funny kind of thing and it is usually defined by the interpretation of an event or happening. If a bird drops from the sky and lands on your head, that is definitely bad luck. If it misses you by inches, then you had good luck. But if that bird falls in the next county, then you don't care and no luck was involved. The act of making your own luck or pushing your luck is also an interpretation that usually depends on the odds of accomplishing or failing a particular task or event. This happens a lot in Snarf's world and drives a lot of the story line. If my character decides to run and leap from one rooftop to another rooftop twelve feet away, this task may be within the realms of my physical abilities. If I make it, then I was lucky. If I don't, then I had bad luck. If my character tries to jump to a rooftop forty feet away, there is no good or bad luck involved; my character is just plain stupid. But if I land on my feet unhurt, then I am darn lucky! Being stupid enough to try something that is just beyond your limits involves stupid luck. Stupid luck can be very funny and add humor to a game. This happens a lot in Snarf's world.

EPISODE #18: FLIGHT FROM KEYNOVIA

The brave crew of the gagglezoomer cart continued their uncontrolled, high-speed ride through Keynovia, crashing right through the Blue Horse Bar—bringing aboard an attractive barmaid and a large jug of wine. They missed the bridge to the north road and went through the river (losing the barmaid but not the wine). Snarf used his head—er, his nose—to get the leech off of the 'zoomer's back. He crawled back toward the cart, knowing that once he lifted his foot off the beast's back, it would come to a stop.

Stop it did. The resulting inertia caused the cart to fly up and stand balanced at a 90-degree angle from the road. Snarf, Aveeare, and Dorque held on for dear life. Dorque's recently acquired wine had been awfully shaken up, though, and the cork popped off, right on the gagglezoomer's back! The cart hit the ground as the huge lizard took off once more, but before the group had time to adjust the cork rolled off its back. This time the 'zoomer had traction, and the cart was flung—loopty-loop fashion—before tumbling to a stop.

The group was reloading the cart when the city guards came running, swords drawn and spears at the ready. "You are under arrest for disturbing the peace, for reckless driving, for destruction of private property, and a list of other crimes." The trio climbed back in the cart and prepared for a quick getaway.

Adventure Notes

Make Them Change Their Minds: Snarf probably never would have set foot in a gagglezoomer cart again, if the Keynovian guards weren't chasing the group. Suddenly the 'zoomer wasn't doom but salvation! Changing the circumstances can make bad options quickly seem appealing.

EPISODE #19: THE PLAINS OF WAFOO (or "So long, Dorque!")

Snarf, Dorque, and Aveeare hit the road with the guards in hot pursuit. Dorque decided to "give dose guards a lil' lip," standing up and insulting the guards, the king—and just when he was really getting going, an overhanging sign knocked him off the cart. A quick decision was made: "Throw all his gear out and wish him good luck!" Snarf and Aveeare made it out of the city, on the Old North Road heading out to the Plains of Wafoo.

On the open road Snarf and Aveeare were able to make excellent time and practice stopping the gagglezoomer. They met the refugees from the city of Quessa, which had been conquered by a "strange man that commands a dragon." The king was taken prisoner and the population enslaved. Aveeare was quite eager to see a dragon… Snarf not so much.

EPISODE #20: LIBERATION OF QUESSA (or "The Return of Suthaze")

Snarf was not interested in chancing an encounter with a dragon, but when the Quessan refugees mentioned great reward and the chance at a beautiful princess' hand in marriage, Snarf had a quick change of heart. At 'zoomer speed, it did not take long to reach Quessa. The zeetvah adventurer decided to charge right into the middle of the city, to "surprise the @*#! out of them."

Charge they did, quite successfully until Snarf lost the gagglestick—just before they reached the city market square filled with hundreds of people and a man standing on the platform. People dived out of the way, and Snarf recognized the man on the platform just before they smashed into it (and him)—it was Suthaze! The gagglezoomer cart smashed everyone into the city wall. Though stunned, only Suthaze was knocked out. They quickly tied the evil wizard up and Aveeare disintegrated Suthaze's staff.

The Quessans were grateful, but told their saviors that Suthaze's dragon still guarded the courtyard. Snarf seemed strangely confident that he and Aveeare could handle the dragon…

EPISODE #21: BABE #2 (or "The Dragon Slayers")

Snarf showed no fear in entering the courtyard, with Aveeare almost certain the zeetvah had gone mad! Snarf was sure, however, that the dragon was Willie, somehow again convinced he was a duck. At first his theory appeared to be wrong and Snarf nearly soiled his breeches, but finally the dragon explained he really was Willie, but "Sthuthaze told me to act like a dragon, real bad and mean. The whole town thinks I'm a dragon… quack!"

Snarf's plan was simple. He told Willie to keep up the make-believe act, and have a "pretend" fight with them before fleeing the city to fly south for the winter. They all put on a spectacular show for the citizens of Quessa, who truly fell for the ruse. Snarf and Aveeare liberated the king, who promised great reward and a feast in the heroes' honor.

Later that evening, the king and his daughter argued about the custom of the princess marrying a hero. She refused outright to marry Snarf, but thought she might consent to marry Aveeare once she saw his face.

EPISODE #22: THE LADY-KILLER (or "Aveeare Flips His Lid")

Aveeare and Snarf got dressed for the celebration feast, both quite excited and looking their best. (The robot wore a quite sporting tie.) The king informed Aveeare that Princess Penelope wished to see him. The robot politely obliged while Snarf continued to primp and preen.

The princess was determined to see Aveeare's face, and that she wanted to give him "like, a royal kiss." (Penelope talks like an 80s valley girl fersure.) She worked quite hard to take Aveeare's "helmet" off, but when the robot protested she settled for him simply opening his visor.

Before the kiss, the princess peeked and saw all of the circuits and gadgetry that made up Aveeare's "face." The sight was too much for Penelope, who screamed and dropped over in a dead faint. Snarf charged in with the king in tow, and Snarf took one look at the robot's "face" and thought it was a mass of scar tissue.

Aveeare was indignant, protesting that his face was "the latest style in robots." This impressed the awakened Penelope, for whom fashion was life. She announced that Aveeare was her chosen hero. She would marry the robot! Snarf was not pleased.

EPISODE #23: THE HEROES DEPART (or "The Cult of Robot Personality")

Snarf was determined not to let another beautiful woman slip away. He began immediately making excuses why Aveeare could not marry Penelope, all of which the robot protested. The king could not understand why Aveeare refused marriage, even after refuting all of Snarf's wild lies. Aveeare not-so-patiently explained: "I cannot eat. I cannot marry. I cannot sleep. I cannot have children… I AM A ROBOT!"

This only impressed Penelope more, who admired Aveeare's devotion to individualism. The king, however, knew he needed an heir. Aveeare was ruled out as husband-material, though Snarf was refused as well—on the grounds that the king did not want grandchildren "runnin' around with long ears and snouts."

Snarf reluctantly agreed. Penelope was heartbroken, but vowed to start a fashion movement modeled after Aveeare. Snarf's disappointment was appeased with a chest full

of treasure, which he soon cashed in for more transportable jewels. Over the next few days, Aveeare was astonished to see how quickly the robot cult took off among Quessa's social elite. Snarf had a portrait commissioned for the Quessa Hall of Heroes. (The artist looks strangely familiar, doesn't he?) Finally the pair loaded up the gagglezoomer cart and headed north, continuing toward the Perpetual Pit.

Adventure Notes

Let Their Actions Come Back to Haunt Them: Aveeare thinks, at this point, that the robot cult is weird but harmless. Later we learn that Penelope starts an entire knighthood based on robotic ideals! The party will take situations much more personally when they feel personally responsible. Give it to 'em!

EPISODE #24: THE PERPETUAL PIT

After three days of searching, Snarf and Aveeare still had not found the Pit. When they did, they nearly drove the gagglezoomer right into it—instead finding themselves dangling at the mercy of the leech, who was holding onto the gagglestick. Snarf promised the leech a fabulous reward for saving their lives. While the zeetvah tried to formulate a plan, two Whazzat lizards wandered by.

Snarf began tossing jewels up, trying to hit the gagglezoomer's back (to make it run and pull them out of the Pit). After a few misses, Snarf's aim improved, but a lizard intercepted and ate the jewels! Finally the zeetvah pulled out the revolver, and at Aveeare's urging he tossed it in a well-lobbed arc. The pistol landed on the gagglezoomer's back. The huge lizard took off at a run, saving Snarf and Aveeare's bacon.

Adventure Notes

Add Complications: The situation in the Pit was dangerous enough without interfering Whazzat lizards, but having the meddling creatures there made things truly desperate. When things seem bad, make 'em worse. Really challenge the characters to get out of the latest mess.

EPISODE #25:
DEATH OF A GAGGLEZOOMER

Snarf and Aveeare had no time to recover before one of the Whazzat lizards grabbed the pistol. The ensuing chase caused the lizard to leap onto the gagglezoomer's back! The 'zoomer cart bounced around, uncontrolled, in the rocky terrain and got completely turned around, heading back toward the Pit.

Snarf had a plan. With the leech on the gagglestick, he told the critter to grab the Whazzat lizard as it passed by. The plan worked—but it was too late, the 'zoomer plunged over the side, falling down the bottomless pit.

Aveeare pleaded mercy for the Whazzat lizard, distracting Snarf by explaining exactly what the gun was and how it worked. The leech, meanwhile, was ticked that Snarf did not keep his promise of a reward. A whack to the snout with the gagglestick got his attention, and Snarf rummaged through his pouch for a reward.

EPISODE #26: ANOTHER WISH

Snarf, in typical greed, tried to go cheap on the leech's reward, ultimately settling on a tiny diamond ring. What the zeetvah didn't know, however, was that the ring was actually a ring of wishing. Because the leech could not speak in order to make the wish, it lamented in frustration "I wish dat I could communicate with everything!" One magical PING later, it was able to talk to a bug (who recognized the leech's true nature as a dark shade death leech!), the lizard, and finally Snarf—who failed to realize it was the leech's new telepathy.

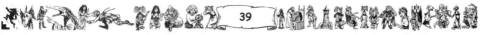

EPISODE #27:
BLESSING AND A CURSE

The leech was pleased as punch over his new-found communicative powers, but was frustrated that Aveeare could not hear him. Hungry, the death leech wandered off to stalk some prey. Unfortunately, it was now able to understand its victim's cries for mercy. It couldn't bring itself to kill, and resolved the crisis of conscience by turning vegetarian, ignoring the apple's screams as it sucked out the juice.

The next morning the rag-tag band set out west. Snarf continued to hear voices, picking up the leech's conversation. Despite warnings from the lizard and the leech, the group was caught surprised by a mountain giant! One swing of the enormous club sent Snarf sailing like a golf ball over of a driving range. Aveeare, the lizard, and the leech regrouped in hiding, afraid that Snarf might be dead!

EPISODE #28: KNOCKED STUPID

Snarf was not dead, but he was clearly not rowing with all oars, either. The zeetvah staggered around, convinced he was made of sound. The leech decided to shut him up: "Snarf, you are a rock!" Snarf was easily persuaded, and huddled down, unmoving (rather like a rock, actually). Aveeare attempted shock therapy to snap Snarf out of it, but that only made Snarf think he was lightning, as he began throwing himself into trees and rocks. The leech tried again: "Snarf, you are a...a gagglezoomer!" Snarf calmed down, but Aveeare—not realizing what the leech had said—tied a rope around Snarf, wanting to secure the crazed zeetvah. The moment the rope touched Snarf's back, he took off on a run! Aveeare followed behind, since Snarf was running straight toward the giant.

EPISODE #29: TELERIE WINDYARM
(or "Third Time's the Charm")

Snarf ran at the giant, bouncing right off its shoulder. The giant, none too bright himself, argued with the zeetvah. ("I'm a gagglezoomer!" "No you ain't!" "Oh yes I am!") The leech, riding on the lizard's back, shouted the first thing he could think of: "Snarf, you are a honey bee!"

From his perch on a giant log, Snarf the bee began "stinging" the giant's belly (with a sword). The giant raised his club high to smash Snarf like a bug, but the "bee" leaped out of the way. The log see-sawed its way into the giant's face, killing it instantly!

Just then, a beautiful, curly-haired warrior-woman approached, calling herself Telerie Windyarm. She had an interesting tale for the group: "There's a legend in this area that says a giant guards a trail that goes up in the mountains where a great treasure is hidden." Snarf, still confused, was eager to take up this new quest.

EPISODE #30: EYES IN THE DARK

Telerie guided the group up the mountain pass, not understanding Snarf's strange behavior. (The zeetvah was still under the delusion that he was a heroic honey bee.) They reached a pitch-black cave. Stumbling around in the dark, they encountered something

that sent everyone running—except Snarf, who blindly began to "sting" in the darkness with his sword. When the group returned with a torch, Snarf saw himself standing nose-to-nose with a horrifying cave beast! Throat-clenching fear snapped the zeetvah back to his senses, and he started to run before Aveeare called out "Wait Snarf! I think it's dead." Snarf had indeed slain the beast, an act that truly impressed Telerie.

Before Snarf could exaggerate his deeds, the leech advised him to "play it cool." Though Snarf did not know where the strange voice came from, he followed its advice and stayed modest, further winning Telerie over. As they proceeded farther in the cave, they saw a light up ahead.

EPISODE #31: GATHGOR'S KEEP

Telerie told the group they were in the Keep of Gathgor, an evil wizard. Snarf was hesitant, but did not want to show fear in front of Telerie. He urged the group on. When they reached a huge door, Telerie warned that it could be trapped. Aveeare X-rayed the lock system and saw it wasn't even locked. Unfortunately he did not check the entire doorframe for traps. A beam shot out from the side of the wall, knocking the robot senseless. Snarf tied Aveeare to the Whazzat lizard and they pressed onward.

Their next encounter was a bugbear guard, who did not intimidate Telerie in the least. "Snarf, I'll take care of this freak myself!! Come on, dude, let's party!" A few expert moves later, Telerie had slain the guard and lost only her helmet in the process. Snarf, the leech, and the lizard were suitably impressed.

EPISODE #32: SPLIT UP!

The party reached a T-junction, with a door straight ahead. Snarf volunteered to open the door—freeing a terrifying spectre! Snarf and Telerie fled to the left, the lizard ran to the right (with the leech riding his back and the unconscious Aveeare in tow). The spectre followed the latter, as Aveeare began to recover while tied to the runaway lizard. When Aveeare saw the spectre, he zapped it with a large electrical blast to disperse the undead spirit.

Meanwhile, Snarf and Telerie found a closet full of clothes. These inspired the maiden warrior, who devised a quick plan.

EPISODE #33: TELERIE'S PLAN (or "Snarf Gets a Peek")

Telerie urged Snarf to dress up like an evil guard, while Telerie changed into the gown of a noblewoman. (The beautiful Telerie was quite willing to strip naked in front of Snarf, giving the zeetvah an eyeful. He realized that Telerie had no sense of modesty.) The two loosely tied rope around Telerie's wrists as if she was a prisoner, with Snarf marching her down

the hall at swordpoint. When they ran into a half-orc guard, they were able to fool him into revealing the location of the "Master's" room.

On the two adventurers' way to ambush Gathgor, a scruffy-looking Trummel emerged from a secret passage. Seeing Snarf, the Trummel drew his sword. "Yeeaa! A slimey guard! Take dis!"

EPISODE #34:
THE WIND-SPLITTING SWORD

Snarf skillfully disarmed the Trummel, who said that he was "Jarp, da best thief in da world." Jarp had helped Aveeare escape down the secret passage, and was planning on robbing Gathgor's treasury. The Trummel promised to help Snarf and Telerie for a share in the treasure.

The trio entered Gathgor's chamber, with Snarf having to shut Jarp up before he ruined the deception. The wizard was not easily fooled, however, recognizing Telerie—who had been seeking vengeance on Gathgor the whole time! Snarf felt betrayed, but Telerie promised she would split the treasure equally.

Jarp thought he could use the commotion to slip into the treasure room, but a magical blast from Gathgor left him as nothing more than a pile of ashes and a pair of bulgy eyeballs. Telerie drew her sword, which glowed with magical power, and used it to deflect Gathgor's magical attacks.

Snarf dove for cover, searching through his pack of holding for the pistol. He drew a flashlight instead, and the bright light distracted the wizard long enough for Telerie to wound him. But Gathgor had enough time to complete his spell and froze Telerie's boots to the floor!

Adventure Notes

Secret Motivations: Not every hero needs to be an open book. Encourage hidden agendas for the characters, then work them into the campaign. It will be a big surprise when the truth comes out.

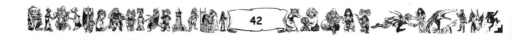

EPISODE #35: TEAMWORK (or "The Leech Strikes Back")

Snarf frantically searched his pack for the pistol. But Gathgor magically yanked the pack out of his hands and across the room. "Run, Snarf!" Telerie cried. Snarf complied, dodging around the chamber and leaping into a huge urn just as Aveeare emerged from a secret passage. Gathgor cast a spell of intense cold on Aveeare, who calmly melted the ice by raising his internal temperature. Snarf, meanwhile, tossed his helmet out and bonked the wizard on the head. Gathgor responded by destroying the urn—thankfully Snarf had already escaped and made his way to Telerie, trying to unlace her boots.

Telerie deflected Gathgor's magic while Snarf worked. Aveeare decided to help, giving Gathgor an electrical blast to the posterior. "Where did all these idiots come from?" the wizard wondered, then threw a blast of fire at Aveeare, succeeded only in burning the robot's coat to cinders. Telerie was finally freed of her frozen boots and made her way toward Gathgor. Snarf retrieved both his pack and the pistol, took aim and fired!

The shot clearly missed, but Gathgor's eyes opened wide in surprise and he fell over—dead. Aveeare found the leech attached to the old wizard's neck, a leech who was irritated that he killed the villain while Snarf got all the credit (as well as affection from Telerie).

EPISODE #36: INTERFACING

The group interred Jarp's ashes in a gold vase, then set about looking for the hidden treasury. It was easily found, and contained vast piles of gold and riches. Telerie was more than pleased: "Snarf…we're rich beyond our wildest dreams!" They filled Snarf's magical pack and a medium-sized chest with all of the most valuable coins and gems.

With a little unacknowledged urging from the leech, the group lowered a rope and climbed out the window and down the mountainside. Later that evening the leech decided to bridge the communication gap between itself and Aveeare. The leech climbed up on the robot's head, concentrated very hard while slipping a tentacle into Aveeare's interface socket. An overwhelming amount of memory flooded the leech's brain. It passed out cold.

The next morning the leech could not be revived, so Snarf tied him to the Whazzat lizard. The group set out again, when a loud roar came from the sky. "Another dragon!!" Snarf exclaimed, but it was another spaceship. Aveeare jumped for joy while Snarf, Telerie, and the lizard all ran in separate directions.

EPISODE #37: HELLO, FRED! (or "Goodbye, Fred!")

Aveeare called out to his friends to come back. "This is not a monster!" A man emerged from the flying ship and spoke to Aveeare in some strange tongue. The strange man (with the pointy ears of an elf) told them he came in response to Aveeare's homing signal. Snarf and Telerie, not understanding the man's techno-speak, did not trust him.

The man, Fred, performed the shut-down procedure on Aveeare in order to remove the homing signal. He turned Aveeare's head 180-degrees. "He broke Aveeare's neck!" Telerie exclaimed. Fred protested, but Telerie socked him in the jaw. Snarf and Telerie tied and gagged Fred, taking their time to decide a method of vengeance.

Telerie spotted a gagglezoomer over in the bushes, and Snarf decided to tie Fred to the 'zoomer, securing the rope down on its back. Snarf bade Fred farewell: "Watch out for rocks an' big trees for da next couple of weeks! Bye-bye!"

Later, the pair prepared to bury their murdered friend. When Snarf pushed in Aveeare's power button, however, the robot came back to "life"—immediately asking his friends: "Where is the man from the ship?"

EPISODE #38: EFFIM

Snarf and Telerie improvised some quick white lies to cover up their actions regarding Fred. Aveeare was certain that Fred became afflicted with space madness. "We will never get him to go back up. We must forget him." Snarf and Telerie were relieved.

Aveeare led the pair into the ship, finding a maintenance robot FM94763-2X817, or "Effim." Effim guided them to Fred's old room, where they changed clothes and relaxed. Suddenly Snarf thought of something: "Telerie, what is today's date?" The answer horrified him, for it was the day before his quest for the throne was up—and he was on the other side of the continent from Zeetville!

Effim had an easily solution. In the morning they would fly to the village in the ship! Snarf and Telerie got into new costumes, had a great meal, and received a crash course in astronomy and the functions of the ship. Morning came, and the ship took off for Zeetville!

EPISODE #39: THE CROWNING CEREMONY

Though the flight did not agree with Snarf's stomach, they quickly reached Snarf's village. He hoped to make a grand entrance, but no one was in town! They followed the noise of a

crowd and found everyone gathered around a platform, complete with a throne. The village elder was about to officially crown one Newfert the Bold as the new king. "STOP! Stop da ceremony!" Snarf screamed. Since Newfert had not yet been crowned, the village elder decided to hear Snarf's claim to the throne.

The villagers were quite impressed with the ship and Snarf's accumulated wealth, and found his story quite amazing. Newfert, however, challenged that because Snarf had no witnesses for the early part of his story, it must be stricken. Snarf thought fast, then asked Aveeare to find Etheah's cottage on the map and retrieve his friends for their testimony.

The village was divided. Snarf decided to go down to the river and see just what Newfert had brought back with him. Newfert's henchman, Sneeve, followed our hero—clearly up to no good.

EPISODE #40: RETURN OF WILLIE

When he looked and saw a dragon chained to a large rock, Snarf was sure he was beaten. But suddenly the dragon looked up and said "Sthnarf, isth dat you? Quack." Yes, it was Willie! Poor Effim tried to stop Sneeve from reporting Snarf's discovery, but Newfert sneaked up and clobbered the little robot.

Newfert and Sneeve then bushwhacked Snarf, tied him in a bag, and hung him from a tree right next to Willie. Sneeve told Willie the bag was full of snakes, and that he must breathe fire "like a real dragon." When Willie balked, Sneeve gave Willie a "magic" rock that would allow him to breathe fire. (Ahem.) Willie began huffing and puffings as he hated to disappoint his friends…

Back at the village, Aveeare returned with none other than Etheah, Raffendorf, and Geezel, who were only too glad to verify Snarf's early adventures. With both Snarf and Newfert presenting a strong claim, the elder declared it would be put up to a vote that evening.

A little zeetvah interrupted Telerie, introducing himself, a little girl, a husband, and wife as Snarf's family! They had thought him dead when he did not return with the other warriors.

EPISODE #41: COMPLICATIONS

Telerie sent Aveeare down to the river to check on Snarf and Effim. The first thing the robot found was poor Effim stuck headfirst in the river. Snarf, meanwhile, woke up tied up and confused inside the sack—the same sack that Willie was desperately trying to ignite with flame breath. When Aveeare approached, recognizing the dragon, Willie found new resolve. "Sthand back boysth! I'll protect youst!" Flame erupted from Willie's mouth setting the bag on fire, which fell into the river. All was quiet except for a few bubbles—then Snarf jumped out of the water, still tied, gagged…and mad!

Snarf returned to the village with tales of Newfert's treachery, plus an explanation that taming Willie was not exactly an extraordinary feat. The villagers and elders began to argue the merits of each case, while Snarf took a moment to meet up with his old friends Etheah, Raffendorf, and Geezel.

In the meantime, a female dragon flew past the area, depressed about her "old maid" status. She was pleased with her sudden turn of luck when she spotted Willie, a good-looking young male. Poor Willie, of course, was terrified at the sight of a dragon. The female took pity on him, determined to avenge him on the zeetvah village. She marched up the hill, almost right into Newfert! "Willie, how did you get outta yer chains?" he said, then ordered "Willie" to act like a mean dragon and return with him to the village. The she-dragon wondered what was going on but played along.

Newfert marched back to the village, with the female dragon following behind. It was an impressive sight. Etheah and Telerie warned Snarf that this exhibition would hurt his case. Snarf was concerned, though, that this dragon did not have the same vacant, glazed look of Willie.

EPISODE #42: THE FINAL SHOWDOWN

Snarf was afraid for the zeetvahs, and quietly begged Newfert to send everyone home. Newfert took advantage of it to reject Snarf's story of being friends with the dragon. To further show his bravery, Newfert instructed the dragon to open her mouth as Sneeve stuck his head inside.

The dragon promptly ended the deception by incinerating Sneeve's head. "All your stupid games are over," she sneered. The villagers fled in panic. During the commotion, Aveeare and Snarf came up with a plan.

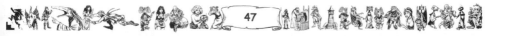

Before Snarf approached the dragon, Telerie, afraid that Snarf was going to get himself killed, confessed her love... er, like for him. This only bolstered Snarf's courage. "Stand back, Telerie, I have a job to do!"

Snarf told the dragon he knew where a great treasure was buried. It was behind many locks and traps, but he had the key. Snarf pulled out the pistol. "I'll g-give you da key, b-but I gotta s-show ya how t-to use it. Jus' l-look down dis lil' pipe." The dragon leaned in, moving her head up against the gun's barrel. BLAM! BLAM! Two gaping holes opened in the dragon's head, and it fell dead to the ground.

A silence came over everything... no one moved. Finally, the village elder loudly proclaimed "Snarf is king!" The coronation ceremony was held that night. Snarf and his friends were at last celebrating the completion of his year-long quest.

And everything was well in zeetville... for now.

The story continues in the graphic novel. They set off on another great adventure in space. They jump through time and go into the future, learn to play rock and roll, drive a truck, mine for gold, meet new people and make new friends!!

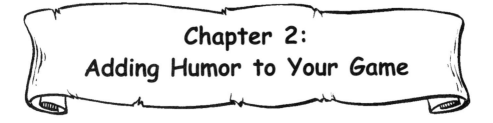

Chapter 2:
Adding Humor to Your Game

New races? Check. Classes? Check. Monsters? Check. How to run funny d20 System games? Well, not only is it a check, you can take this chapter to the bank. Proceed for SnarfQuest gaming secrets worth their value in gold that no self-respecting zeetvah would pass up!

SERIOUS WORLD VS. COMEDY

SnarfQuest is actually grounded in the conventions of traditional fantasy. The young farm-boy going off to seek fame and fortune through adventure, evil wizards commanding monstrous henchmen, and beautiful maidens waiting to be rescued are all staples of the genre.

What makes things different in SnarfQuest is the bizarre situations and twists on the convention. The young farm-boy is a long-snouted anthropomorphic "hero" with greed as his primary motivation. The evil wizard rides a motorcycle, and the fair maiden turns out to be a nut-job fashion slave. While most of the trappings are the same as conventional fantasy, the plots veer off in strange directions, with the heroes doing most unheroic things—all in the name of funny storytelling.

LOW FANTASY VS. HIGH FANTASY

High fantasy is epic, save-the-world stuff, in which rings are pitched into volcanoes and lances are used to slay mighty dragons. Low fantasy heroes have much more down-to-earth goals, like getting rich, getting the girl, and not getting arrested. Low fantasy heroes are generally more pragmatic in their world-outlook, willing to compromise traditional ethics to get the job done.

SnarfQuest is a world of low fantasy. Snarf is a hero, of that there is no doubt—but he's clearly out for his own interests, and is not above lying, cheating, or fighting dirty to get what he wants. Even his mightiest moment (the slaying of the dragon) was more about clever planning than any ridiculous notions of "honorable combat." He's a working class hero, one who is much easier to identify with and find highly amusing.

Although I didn't illustrate this in the strip, I feel that Snarf was just an average guy, or Zeetvah. I imagine him being around 25 years old, living with his family, and doing odd jobs to make himself some spending money. He had no exceptional skills, and he wasn't even a warrior, he was just average! He dreamed of being rich and changing his life from boring to exciting. He had no debts, no wife and kids, no responsibilities. So when the opportunity of becoming king came along, he jumped on it.

When Snarf is in any tight situation he does what any average guy would do to save his hide. He would scheme, lie, cheat, and fight, only when he has to or has the advantage. When all else fails, he runs away as fast as he can. I feel that all my characters in the comic strip acted as normal people would in most of the situations that occurred. I didn't really create any larger than life characters, no superheroes or anyone too powerful. It is more fun that way.

HUMOROUS GAMING

A humorless SnarfQuest DM is as useful as a claustrophobic astronaut. But since you made it this far, it's safe to assume nobody has to put a goofy mask on you to pretend you're amusing. We'll just point out a few things that separate SnarfQuest from low-brow slapstick here. Pay attention, young zeetvahs, if you hope to emulate King Snarf's escapades. There may be a test later. Lowest score gets sixteen flips on da back of dat ol' 'zoomer, on a hundred yards of limestone road.

SNARFQUEST MAXIM #1:

THE SILLIEST POSSIBLE THING THAT CAN HAPPEN, WILL!

In an ordinary game, when you dive into a pond to escape a formidable foe and score a critical success for the skill check, the DM just rules that you hide too well to be spotted. In any normal campaign, if you roll a 1 while attacking, the DM simply dismisses it as a bad miss.

Not so in a SnarfQuest adventure, where an accidental bug-in-the-faceplate can ruin a pursuer's day, and a stray bullet can detonate a whole castle. Even a seemingly trivial action can lead to spectacular consequences. It is that unpredictable whim, akin to stomping someone's toe when he's fully expecting a roundhouse, that lends the comic's humor.

But most—and we dare say all—of the hijinks are impossible to preplan for a game, since the best comedy comes from spontaneity. As the DM, you can prepare "goofy" encounters from now till Dorque Da Wanderer earns a Ph.D. in nuclear physics, and still see them drop deader than fat cows at a gaggaleech convention. However, you can inspire the players to chip in. After all, they know what tickles their funnybones. It's the difference between trying to force a pie in their face, and them willingly taking one for laughs.

SNARFQUEST MAXIM #1.5:

AFTER THE SILLIEST POSSIBLE THING HAPPENS, ANOTHER WILL FOLLOW.

King Snarf's incredulous, anything-goes saga is filled with one crazy turn after another. It means Murphy's Law is always in motion. As the comic's creator Larry Elmore explained, "I just try to think of a logical flow of events, then find a stupid way to arrive at the same conclusions."

That is the perfect advice for running a SnarfQuest game. Ask the question, "What is the goofiest thing to insert here?" Of course, your answer may vary—Raffendorf's foot stuck in a hole might become his head buried in a beehive in your game. Whenever there's a predicament, it's a chain of "stupid" things waiting to happen. Build on it with something equally absurd, if not worse than the previous event. Logic has no place here; if it did, Aveeare with his "mangled" face would have never attracted a cute princess, much less a cult following! Never let dice decide for you when an outcome should be funny. Would Willie the Duck be as hysterical if he's given and made a saving throw to avoid amnesia after Suzthaze's castle exploded? No, you'll just end up losing one of the best gags in the comic.

> Each month when I did the comic strip, I had a general plan of how I wanted the direction of the plot and story to go. For example; I wanted the story to move from point A to point B. Of course there would be a simple way, like just walk from one town to another. But I would take in to consideration the personalities of the characters and throw in some luck, usually bad, and come up with the silliest way they could move from A to B.

SNARFQUEST MAXIM # 2:

IT'S BETTER TO BE LUCKY THAN GOOD. MUCH BETTER.

Dumb luck is a SnarfQuest hero's best friend. The same should happen in your game as well.

The characters ought to be bumbling through the adventure, grabbing the wrong items, taking the wrong turn, always running into one trouble after another. That means they should never be allowed time to plan. No ten-minute break to discuss combat strategy. No huddles to fret over how to divide the loot. No filibusters aboutwhich direction to go. Anybody wasting more than 30 seconds to debate is automatically caught flat-footed and the opinion voided.

Balancing the hair-trigger pace is that in the end, all their decisions, even random, mindless ones, should unfailingly turn out for the best. What the characters lacked in abilities, it's the DM's duty to doubly compensate for in good fortune. If a character is separated from the rest, he will reunite with his companions at the most opportune time, perhaps fortuitously foul up a pursuer (slamming open a door in his face), provide auspicious distraction (shining a flashlight into an opponent's eyes), break into a long-winded soliloquy ("Your evil is no match for my superior blah blah blah…"), or generally save the day (blowing a dragon away with a chance shot from a gun). And who said they need the map to find their way, anyway? There'll be a coincidence or two to usher them along, since Lady Luck, wearing a blindfold, is perpetually there to lead them through clutch moments.

For non-dice roll situations, this requires the DM to think on his feet. You'll find that familiarity with the characters and their history often comes in handy. Any old acquaintances or forgotten plots can be rehashed to conveniently bridge the current dilemma and tie up two loose ends at once. It can also serve as a DM's "mouthpiece" and springboard to adventure.

When it comes to dice rolls, be lenient in crunch time. Fudge a roll if the outcome is going to be too grim or "too real." Err on the side of overprotecting the characters. Better still, give bonuses for actions that draw laughter from other players or yourself, predicated on how funny it will make the scene. Conversely, penalize actions that can be construed as "serious" or just flat-out uninteresting, wargaming-like.

Dumb luck also protects a main character from serious injuries. You won't see blows that would fall a mortal man snuffing the light out of the Good Guys, or a recurring villain like Suthaze. Rather, they simply get "knocked silly."

SNARFQUEST MAXIM # 2.5:

IT'S NEVER LUCK IN YOUR STORY.

And you're sticking to it.

If you don't talk up your daring-dos, nobody will. SnarfQuest is about spreading words of your deed as much as… well, being how ridiculously fortunate you were but never let on. Including taking credits for things you didn't do that you thought you could've done but not sure if you really did. Kind of like how Snarf got the props for killing Gathgor, when the leech just happened to be hanging off his neck.

Recounting the misadventures (but leaving out the "mis" part) in glorious detail to convince the locals of your heroic virtues (i.e., "brag") should be routine for every SnarfQuest character. Encourage the players to tell tall-tales of their characters every chance they get.

Should you care if they lie like a cheap rug? No! It's part of making them bigger than life. Egg them on with awed, wide-eyed peasants clamoring for more, while it gets stranger and more exaggerated down the line! Of course, they must inevitably face the price of their own fame by fighting greater threats, go on bigger quests with higher stakes… something about responsibilities, power, and all that jazz. (You can have the object of their brag—"I killed dat ole ogre single-handed with nottin' but my camp-spoon!"—suddenly show up to enjoy the story, too!)

SNARFQUEST MAXIM #3

IT'S ALL ABOUT STYLE.

Take a blundering anthromorphic buffoon. Please. How cool is he if he loses the treasure all the time, pulls annoying shenanigans, and never ends up with the girl? Why, he's playing a bit part right now in a juggernaut movie franchise having to do with a little kid who became a badass villain in a dark helmet.

The difference between a flaming fool and a respectable one (such as Snarf) is simply S-T-Y-L-E. Yes, Snarf is silly. Yes, Snarf is lucky. But he also has the flair of a hero when the chips are down… well, at least he knows how to take full advantage of his triumphs and conducts himself like a true conquering hero.

Which is important to the DM because the campaign will degenerate into a morass of cornball adventures and inept comic relief if it is not supported with the staple and panache of heroic fantasy; you know, the fair maiden to be won, the evil mages and his minions to be overcome, the sumptuous feast and the generous reward afterward.

That is the SnarfQuest strip in essence, classic fantasy plots with humorous twists in between the beginning and the end. There may be bizarre humanoids for sight gags or merged stereotypes (the valley-girl Princess Penelope) for unexpected levity, but the heroes never came across as completely incompetent nincompoops, even if they needed some luck here and there (okay, lotsa luck). Unless a character is intentionally played as a foolish second-fiddle to the party, he should be accorded all proper respect due real heroes. The characters must be opportunistic, but only if the DM is willing to give them the opportunity.

SNARFQUEST MAXIM #3.5:

GOING MEDIEVAL IS NOT THE ONLY WAY TO STYLE

The SnarfQuest world is eclectic. The principal theme is fantasy, but the liberal sampling of other genres contributes greatly to its unique humor. It regularly introduces elements that the characters aren't familiar with, but we as readers are hip to. Trying to make sense of such peculiarities as motorcycle, robot, and spaceship from a medieval perspective generated many laughs in SnarfQuest.

This is the good old "fish out of water" device, where one attempts to interact in an alien environment or with strange stimuli, and vice versa. The comedy comes from the culture clash. There's always something funny about someone trying to figure out a computer, a cigarette lighter, or something else new for the first time. So it is with the comic strip, as Snarf struggled to comprehend Aveeare, who in turn marveled at such "miracles" as magic.

A SnarfQuest DM can apply the same anachronism to inspire hilarity. How the characters relate and justify the "oddities" from their view will often lead to droll moments, made funnier because the players themselves are in on the joke, much like laughing at "someone" puzzling over the working of a computer (or, on a risqué scale, Telerie's lingerie).

Back to style. While medieval folks will certainly find shades, guitar, and other such accessories fascinating, would they realistically accept them as fashionable? Answer: Who cares? We ourselves see them as cool in real life, therefore they are cool in the game! Here's the bottom line: As long as the game balance isn't upset, let them be the trendsetters and pop icons with their knick-knacks!

VARIANT RULES

Below are a list of varient rules that will add some fun times to any game. Choose only the rules that you feel comfortable with. Its best to start with one or two varient rules and add more once the players get acquainted to the world—remember, too much wahoo can make a game seem to chaotic too be fun! Use these varient rules sparingly! We warned ya!

—BAFFLE THE ENEMY
In game, there is a benefit for acting silly: It tends to dumbfound the enemy. Every time a character does something humorously absurd, whether by luck or intentional, the foe must roll a Wisdom check (DC 12). MAKING the save means he is trying to actually comprehend and make sense of the character's antics, that he is stunned for one round! Only one attempt to "dumbfound" a target per round is permitted, and he will never fall for the same trick twice (at least in the same encounter).

—BRAGGING EXPERIENCE AWARDS
Adventure experience points can only be applied to a character after he has told a group of people (suitability determined by the DM) about the adventure. Story awards for dramatic embellishment should be applied accordingly.

—CRITICALLY FAILED ABILITY CHECKS

The following results happen on any natural "1" rolled for an ability check.

•*Strength:* You throw your back out and are completely immobile for 2d6 minutes.

•*Dexterity:* You manage to knock yourself unconscious for 2d6 minutes.

•*Constitution:* You are completely winded and are stunned for 2d6 minutes.

•*Intelligence:* You are absolutely convinced of something completely wrong for 2d6 minutes.

•*Wisdom:* You cannot make any Wisdom-based skill checks for 2d6 minutes.

•*Charisma:* You lose your composure and cannot make any Charisma-based skill checks for 2d6 minutes. For example, no one is pretty when they cry.

—EVERYTHING BLOWS UP

If there's even the slightest chance of something exploding, it will. All damage to structures and objects is automatically doubled, however, most characters will miraculously survive the blast!

—EXTREME CRITICAL SUCCESS AND FAILURE

Normally a "natural" 1 or 20 means an automatic failure or success, respectively. This variant goes beyond that, meaning that a 1 indicates a catastrophic failure while a roll of 20 indicates spectacular success. The referee should use his imagination, and let the players have some input, into just how the roll plays out—be it an attack, a skill roll, or saving throw. Reward humorous suggestions bonus experience points.

—KNOCKED SILLY

On a critical hit vs. player characters or a pivotal NPC, the damage is taken off the Intelligence ability, not hit points, to a minimum of 1. Such losses reduce the character's Intelligence modifier correspondingly. The character recovers lost Intelligence at the rate of 1 per hour, but the DM may allow a Will saving throw (DC 12) for instant full recovery for comedy purpose. (In the comic, it's Snarf's "mental shock" from seeing the terrible cave monster).

The referee may impose any and all "zany" consequences on the character, including delirium ("I'm a bee!"), incoherent babbling (great for random spellcasting), and high susceptibility to suggestions ("Um, why don't you let me use that Wand of Wi...I mean, pretty stick for a while").

—THE BEAUTIFUL AND EVERYONE ELSE

This is Larry Elmore's world, so people living in it are either good looking or butt ugly—makes it easy to tell the good from the bad. With this rule, all adult humanoid characters (i.e. standard Core Rulebook I character races) place either their highest roll or lowest on Charisma, thus becoming one of the good looking ones orpart of the ugly!

EVEN MORE TIPS

These ideas go beyond the specific formula of SnarfQuest, and can be used for humorous gaming of any kind.

It's Called Slapstick! A lot of the comedy is physical, and while the d20 System can easily be "miss, hit, hit, miss, roll a save," you should be describing like a half-drunk play-by-play commentator at a little league game gone wrong. Swords should fly out of fighter's hands, wizard spells go off with unforeseen side-effects, and thieves might slip on banana peels. While you're at it, put the energy into your refereeing performance. Get up from that chair and move around, don't be afraid to raise your voice and talk fast. Pantomime some of the weird action with your own body!

Pacing, Pacing, Pacing! The pace of your game should be like a boulder rolling down a hill—getting faster and faster until it crashes into something at the end. One crazy encounter should barrel into another and ricochet off of another wacky situation. This doesn't give the players much time to think—which is good, because it provides fuel for the comedy. (Consider imposing a time limit—say, 3 seconds—for them to make a decision. Keep a stopwatch handy!)

Throw in Running Gags! Snarf's rejection by women, Willie the dragon who thinks he's duck, the gagglezoomer—these are the running gags of SnarfQuest. Your game should have its own signature running gags, with enough variations to keep the players on their toes.

Have No Shame! You set the stupidity bar at your gaming table. If you dare to act like an idiot, they won't be ashamed to do the same. Use goofy voices, cross your eyes, and discard every shred of dignity. You won't be sorry (unless you're being filmed).

There is a lot of slapstick comedy involved with the SnarfQuest strip. Because most of the characters are "normal" people they do not have great power to simply solve extreme situations, so "stuff happens!" Even Suthaze the wizard, though he may be capable of casting some powerful spells, is not a "super" wizard and, like real life, nothing goes exactly as planned. Taking these facts into consideration, I would build a scene where something went wrong, and again, like real life, this would lead to something else happening, which would lead to an even greater event. It is sort of like a car wreck in slow motion. You start to loose control, you try to steer your way out, then you hit oil, then you go off the road backwards at a hundred miles an hour and down a steep hill but your luck may change and you don't hit a tree, you just run through a heard of sheep which cushions your wreck and you survive. Some events you just have to ride out. During all of this you are fighting like mad to save your life and when it is over, and you survive, you realize there were a lot of laughs.

GOOFY NEW FEATS

These feats are separate from those in the Characters chapter because they are completely optional and applicable only in a humorous campaign where the DM feels comfortable using them.

GUESS [General]

You are able to come up with wild ideas that just seem to work.

Prerequisites: Int 13 or less

Benefit: A character can make use of this feat once every hour, providing a +4 competence bonus to any untrained skill check.

GOOD GUY INITIATIVE [General]

You're a hero who seems to have a knack for getting the jump on evil-doers.

Prerequisites: Good Alignment

Benefit: In any conflict in which the majority of your foes are evil, you gain a +2 circumstance bonus to your Initiative check.

Special: This stacks with other feats that grant bonuses to initiative.

INSPIRE SOLILOQUY (or "Before I kill you, Mr. Pond…" Feat)

Villains cannot kill you without telling you their entire evil plan.

Prerequisites: Good Alignment

Benefit: When an evil-aligned creature of Intelligence of 12+ attacks you, roll a Bluff check opposed by a Will saving throw. Success for you means the villain will not attack you for 2d4 rounds, all the while he is telling you his evil plan (or life story). This effect is cancelled if you attack him.

JUST MISSING THE VITALS (or "It's just a Flesh Wound!" Feat)

You often survive attacks that would kill a lesser hero.

Benefit: When a critical threat is scored against you, roll a Reflex saving throw (DC equal to the unmodified attack roll) to simply turn it into a standard hit with regular damage.

FAST HEALER (or "I'm Not Dead Yet!" Feat)

You heal wounds and recover from fatigue at twice the rate of normal people.

Benefit: Your character heals both hit points and subdual damage at the twice the normal rate.

SILVER TOUNGE (or "Talking Crap" Feat)

You are the master of a quickly-told lie.

Benefit: When a character is threatened with immediate danger, he receives a +4 competence bonus to his Bluff checks used to talk his way out of trouble. Difficulty Classes and opponents' Sense Motive checks are rolled normally.

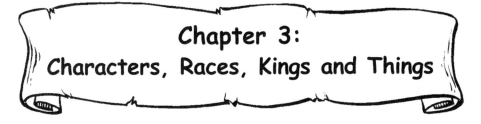
CHARACTER RACES IN SNARFQUEST

The races of the world revealed in SnarfQuest combines standard fantasy fare with the truly bizarre. Ordinary humans meet up with their anthropomorphic counterparts on a regular basis. In fact, in this young world, mankind has not yet gained dominance but is just another race struggling to survive and thrive.

Many of the races in the world of SnarfQuest are those found in the D&D Core Rulebook I. For those races, only information relevant to the setting is included here. The new races presented in this book (and revealed in the pages of the comic) are just a small sampling of what might be out there. So little of the world is explored, and so many races are largely unknown, nearly any beast might have evolved rudimentary intelligence and culture. Many of these live in isolated areas, cut off from other lands until explorers and adventurers come their way. Who knows what sort of furry, feathered, or scaly people could be waiting beyond the next mountain range?

I love to create little critters, new creatures that you have never seen before. I think they are more interesting. Of course, when I am illustrating the creature then you can see them immediately and understand some of their personality. When running a game that is not so easy, unless you are an artist and can simply draw some new ones. Sometimes I would use an existing animal and give it character.

Raffendorf was a giant rat, but in reality, he was a human. B.B. Bird looked like a bird but wasn't. I did a special issue of SnarfQuest once, in Dragon Magazine, that was full of all types of birds and bats that were under a spell by an old wizard. The birds were around 3 feet tall, walked upright and talked. They also had human type characteristics like Snarf.

So the sky is the limit! If you want to use a normal animal as a character, give it some personality, possibly some clothes, and make a real character out of him. At the moment in the new SnarfQuest strip I am doing, I am using my own dog, Max, as a character. He walks upright and talks, but he still has a dog's mentality.

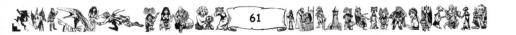

Table 1.1: **New Racial Ability Adjustments**

Race	Ability Adjustments	Favored Class
Almeer, Mean	+2 Strength, -2 Intelligence, -2 Charisma	Barbarian
Almeer, Nice	-2 Strength, +2 Charisma	Sorcerer
Pelfric	+2 Constitution, -2 Strength	Bard
Trummel	+2 Dexterity, -2 Constitution, -2 Strength	Rogue
Zeetvah	+2 Dexterity,-2 Strength	Fighter

ALMEER

Almeers are one of the eldest races in the world, originally fierce tribes of angry brutes—competing with orcs for territory and matching their savagery. When a tribe grew too large, it would split into smaller tribes with different factions following a new leader. The in-fighting of the almeer prevented them from conquering other races, though their tendency to form new tribe has spread members across the continent. In the last few hundred years, however, new kinds of almeer have emerged. Smaller, weaker, and more intelligent, the "nice" almeers have split off and formed several new tribes, but their numbers are far less than the "mean" variety.

Personality: Mean almeers are angry savages. On a good day, they seem like school-yard bullies looking for lunch money. On a bad day, they break into berserking fits before they roll out of the bed. Nice almeers are far more passive and characterized by their curiosity.

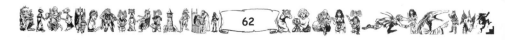

Mean almeers have little sense of community and society, acting on a "might makes right" mentality. They divide a tribe into gang-like factions, each rallying around a strong warrior. The strongest warriors battle for the right to be chieftain. When one chief rules for too long, younger gang-leaders will break away and form new tribes (almost always later making war upon their "parent" tribe).

GEEZEL KNOWS WHERE IT IS! YOU FOLLOW GEEZEL... ME IS SMART... YES ME IS ...(GULP)

Nice almeers have developed small utopian tribes, in which each member has an equal voice in the group's decisions. Work and responsibility is also divided evenly. This offshoot of almeers has remained small enough (usually thanks to their larger cousins) that no major problems have occurred.

Physical Description: Mean almeers are both taller and stronger than humans. An almeer's body is covered in lightly covered fur, ranging from a dusty gold to dark brown (with rare specimens of pure white or black). Almeers possess extremely large eyes that glow in low-light conditions in feline manner. Their mouths are vaguely beak-like, with rows of sharp teeth. The shape of their mouth gives almeers a natural smile—one that mean almeers spend a lifetime contorting into a sinister scowl. An almeer's nose is little more than two tiny nostrils above his mouth. The most distinguishing feature of an almeer is his ears, which are large and splayed out from the side of his head. Mean almeers often have scarred, mutilated, or missing ears from many battles, and to have kept one's ears in good condition is either the sign of a dangerous warrior (for an older almeer) or a unblooded youngster.

Nice almeers resemble their cousins but on a much smaller scale, averaging slightly higher than four-and-a-half feet tall. The muscular build sported by mean almeers is replaced with a more slender frame. The natural smile is worn without shame. While mean almeers go about almost naked, the nice variety tends to adopt some form of clothing—either home-spun or acquired through barter with other races.

All almeers have life-spans shorter than humans, and mature more rapidly.

Relations: Tribes of mean almeers that come in contact with other races invariably try to make war upon them, sometimes obtaining victory and wealth for the tribe, other times calling doom down upon them. Nice almeers shy away from outside contact as a group, while individual almeers are known to venture off and make their way into other civilizations. Aspiring almeer spellcasters seek out experienced wizards and sorcerers to enhance their own knowledge of the magical arts.

Alignment: Mean almeers are chaotic and evil by nature. They believe that the strongest will survive their harsh way of life, and that death is better than living on weakly. Considering this, it is amazing the smaller nice almeers have endured the numerous attempts by their cousins to end their "weak" existence. Nice almeers are usually neutral or neutral good in their disposition.

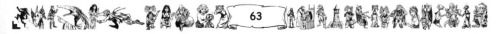

Religion: The larger, mean almeers are convinced that the natural forces of the world are controlled by Grol, a fierce and uncaring deity who values only strength and ferocity. Grol imparts no powers himself, but some shamans revere the mighty wind or the roaring fire and are granted spells. Nice almeers are open-minded about religion, and are slowly learning the beliefs of other cultures.

Language: If the almeers ever possessed a language of their own, they have long since forgotten it, having adopted a crude pidgin of the common tongue and several other languages. Nice almeers have attempted to master Common and speak it as well as humans, though they often carry a thick accent, a lisp, or some other impediment to make them sound less intelligent than they truly are.

Names: "Mean" almeers almost universally use one-syllable names typically ending with hard sounds, names that change through the course of their lives to reflect important events and deeds. "Nice" almeer have longer names that they keep for life. Neither race make distinctions between male and female names.

"Mean" almeer: Bruk, Grik, Kror, Tek, Zort.

"Nice" almeer: Aevil, Denvy, Geezil, Morteen, Samree.

Adventurers: "Mean" almeer are not typically very nice to the younger members of the tribe. Some of these mistreated youths run away, and as social creatures (crude, angry social creatures with violent tendencies) they might very well join up with a new "tribe" of adventurers. Mean almeer have a hard time understanding the rules of civilization or the structure of an adventuring party, leading to many misunderstandings. "Nice" almeer often go out into the world to explore and learn (often pursuing magical studies). Such an individual will happily join an adventuring party, often surprising the group with quick wit and unexpectedly clever solutions to problems.

"MEAN" ALMEER RACIAL TRAITS

+2 Strength, -2 Intelligence, -2 Charisma: These brutal almeers are large and strong yet stupid and crude.

Medium-size: As Medium-size creatures, "mean" almeers have no special bonuses or penalties due to their size.

"Mean" almeers' base speed is 30 feet.

Automatic Language: Common. Bonus Languages: Gnoll, Goblin, and Orc. The more intelligent almeers (which may or may not be saying much) may know the languages of allies or rivals.

Superior hearing: Almeers receive a +2 racial bonus to all Listen checks.

Bite: As a full-attack action, an almeer may bite with its sharp teeth. The bite attack is made at its normal melee attack bonus and inflicts 1d4 points of damage, plus Strength bonus.

Favored Class: Barbarian. A multiclass "mean" almeer's barbarian class does not count when determining whether he suffers an XP penalty. Primitive and driven by rage, "mean" almeer are naturally savage warriors.

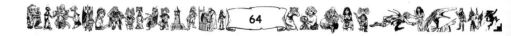

"NICE" ALMEER RACIAL TRAITS

-2 Strength, +2 Charisma: "Nice" almeers are weak in body but strong-willed. They have forceful personalities, yet can also be quite charming when necessary.

Small: As Small creatures, "nice" almeers gain a +1 size bonus to Armor Class, a +1 size bonus on attack rolls, and a +4 size bonus on Hide checks, but they must use smaller weapons than those used by Medium-size creatures, and their carrying limits are three-quarters of a Medium-size character.

"Nice" almeers' base speed is 20 feet.

Automatic Language: Common. Bonus Languages: Elven, Dwarven, Gnome. "Nice" almeers make an effort to learn the languages of the more civilized races of the world.

Superior hearing: Almeer receive a +2 racial bonus to all Listen checks.

Fleet-footed: "Nice" almeers, though slower at walking speed, may run up to five times its normal movement. If a "nice" almeer character later takes the Run feat, it may run up to six times its base movement and gain the additional benefits for jumping as listed in the feat.

Favored Class: Sorcerer. A multiclass "nice" almeer's sorcerer class does not count when determining whether he suffers an XP penalty. Strong-willed and naturally talented in magic, many almeers pursue magical knowledge.

DWARVES

Mountain- and hill-dwelling dwarves are not particularly common in the old young lands, though everyone has heard of them. The underground fortress city of Drevenwo is the most famous home of the dwarves, with smaller clans scattered about. Reclusive and largely untrusting of other races, dwarves generally never venture far from home. Dwarven adventurers are rare, and not typical examples of their kind. Dwarves who do travel are still usu-

When I first started gaming, I always played a dwarf fighter. I found this type of character was more like my own personality and I had fun with him. I wouldn't hesitate to backstab our party's thief if I thought he was stealing from me or from any of our group. Actually I attacked him several times, but before I could ever kill him or he kill me, the rest of the group would pull us apart or hold me back. My old character would attack anyone that pissed him off. But usually the old dude didn't attack anyone that could kill him quickly or easily. When something had to be done that was very risky or dangerous, my character, the most expendable, was always sent in first. I played him as fearless, a little crazy, and a little stupid, but always with a good sense of humor.

ally prone to grumbling, complaining, and occasional agoraphobia.

ELVES

The "fair folk," as they are sometimes called, live in sylvan settings, constructing picturesque cities and towns that blend in so well to the forest terrain that they are not easily found unless one knows what to look for. The huge woodland cities of Nimgalie and Cragengal are spoken of by travelers, though most humans will go their entire lives without ever hearing even the names. Elves are often interested in the world and other races, roaming the lands and cities of other races, sometimes even settling there. The elves have a wide-eyed curiosity and are extremely interested in new places and new experiences. Such tendencies easily thrust adventuring elves into dangerous situations from which their comrades must rescue them!

GNOMES

Not really known for craftsmanship or inventing in the young lands, gnomes have scattered clans that live in burrows and tunnels. They often live near dwarves, trading food and trade goods. (Dwarves, on the other hand, seem to only tolerate gnomes as "middle-men" so they do not have to deal with humans and elves for trade. Gnomes are smart enough to make a sizeable profit from this arrangement.) Usually content to live comfortably in their burrows, the trait that sometimes drives a gnome to adventure is their penchant for practical jokes. Sometimes such pranks go too far, and dwarves (or the gnome's own family) drive him out into the world. With their natural talent for illusion magic, traveling gnomes have a reputation as tricksters and con artists.

HALFLINGS

The small folk called halflings are largely unknown in the western lands. The present clans dwell in the foothills of the Red Mountains, largely isolated from the other races. Smaller groups have migrated to the west, but these are rare. Halflings have received a bad reputation among the westerners who have heard of them, chiefly because several adventuring halflings have been robbers and spies. Most halfings are peaceful, agreeable folk who resent the preconceived notion that they are a race of thieves.

HALF-ELVES

Many elves have immigrated to human cities. Open-minded and intrigued by those different from themselves, elves of The old young lands will have relations with members of other races. While it is rare for an elf to actually marry during such a courtship, they do not understand the reason to "wait" for marriage. The children of these unions are half-elves. Half-elves are normally raised in human cities, though rarely one might be born to an elf returning home. People are more accepting than they will become in later ages, and half-elves do not suffer any particular discrimination—though they sometimes have a difficult time "finding themselves" during adolescence. Many half-elves become adventurers, as the drive of their human blood and the inborn curiosity of the elves drives them out into the world.

HALF-ORCS

Orcs are unpleasant brutes. Though centered around their "city" of Barutoo in the Beast Mountains, orcs have spread throughout The old young lands in small tribes. Outcast orcs sometimes try to find solace in other cultures' acceptance—just as a human barbarian may discover sanctuary in an orc tribe. Relationships between humans and orcs lead to half-orcs, a race usually at odds with itself. Half-orcs combine the brutality of their orcish blood with the intelligence and cunning of their human heritage—a dangerous combination. Half-orcs, though rare in the world, often become adventurers since they are not easily accepted anywhere. Many wander the world, hoping to find somewhere on the road someone who will offer them a hand in friendship.

HUMANS

Though they will grow to become the dominant race of the world, in the ancient young lands the human race is just one of the many trying to survive. While their presence is wide, the human population is thin. Most human settlements are small enough that a natural disaster, plague, or horde of mean almeers can spell the end for it. Humans are not easily discouraged, however, and abandoned settlements do not remain empty for long. Adventuring appeals to many humans who find travel, excitement, and the prospect for wealth and success are worth the danger.

PELFRIC

The pelfrics are one of the many stranger races to appear in The Beast Mountains during the last centuries. Not bird, reptile, or mammal, they are not wide-spread or well-known to other races. Pelfric communities are not well-organized, yet somehow manage to meet basic needs for survival.

Personality: Pelfrics seem, on the surface, to be easy-going and good-natured. They pursue the finer pleasures in life, such as good food, music, and items of luxury. When most day-to-day problems surface, a pelfric will just "let it be" and accept the outcome. Pelfrics are not pacifists, however, and will defend themselves when threatened.

Physical Description: At first glance, many mistakenly assume that a pelfric is some kind of bird. In reality, pelfrics are difficult to classify. A pelfric's large, curved beak certainly resembles that of a bird, as does the shape of its head, neck, and torso. Yet a pelfric has fur, not feathers, that is usually bright in color on a male and more muted colors on a female. Pelfrics have very human looking arms and hands, except they are covered in fur. Smaller than humans, pelfrics are roughly the same height as zeetvahs, though their bodies are lighter.

Pelfrics are not long-lived, the most ancient among them are just over sixty years of age. Though warm-blooded, pelfrics lay eggs and must nest for three months in the manner of birds. Pelfrics are omnivores. They prefer meat and do not feel any special kinship with birds.

Relations: There are only a few villages of pelfrics littered throughout the Beast Mountains. They have very little contact with outside races, though a wanderer may find his way to other races in the western regions. Zeetvahs and "nice" almeers have met up with the pelfrics, though humans and elves will likely never see the bird-like race. Pelfrics' easy-going nature helps them get along well with others.

Alignment: Pelfrics are chaotic and good as a whole, although individuals can vary. Because of the strong commitment to individual ideas and notions, pelfric villages do not strongly insist on a universal moral code. As long as an individual does not hurt anyone else, they don't see the need to force a belief system on anyone. Those who continually hurt others will be kicked out, while someone committing an extreme offense (such as murder) might be put to the sword.

Religion: Pelfrics are somewhat agnostic, understanding that there are greater powers but also believing mortals cannot truly understand them—so why try? Only the most rare pelfrics become clerics or druids, and even these possess an extremely vague faith without many rules. Pelfrics accept that other cultures have more structured beliefs than their own, but don't get too "worked up" about religion.

B.B. Bird is not a bird and does not consider himself one, even though most everyone else thinks he is. I see his race as a missing link between dinosaurs and modern day birds. Sometime during the evolution of the Pelfric race, they developed fur and intelligence, but kept their beaks. There are types of animal species now in our present time that have beaks and are not birds. Pelfrics, like B.B. Bird, find it insulting to be called a bird, but they are used to it and usually don't say much about it unless teased. Then you may have a fight on your hands.

Language: Like other civilizations in the Beast Mountains, pelfrics speak Common. Wandering pelfrics seem to have a knack for language, and can learn the tongues of other races and cultures quite easily. Their bird-like mouth is able to reproduce sounds far outside the abilities of humans, elves, and their ilk, so a pelfric can learn to speak very alien languages if presented the chance.

Names: Pelfric adults have two names. The first name is given by the parents to newly-hatched child, while a second is granted when one becomes an adult. Both names are long, hard to pronounce, and extremely private for anyone outside the pelfric village. When dealing with others, they simply abbreviate their names and add a "last" name which is simply the name of their village. (Known village names include Bird village and Bug town, as well as East and West Egg.) Examples include: B.B. Bird, H.G.W. Egg.

Adventurers: Although not especially motivated to leave home for adventure's sake, pelfrics are always seeking bigger and better things. Some aim to improve their skills and make a name for themselves in the world, while others just want to taste the finest wines and dine in the most exclusive restaurants. They enjoy the company of others, and will join an adventuring party just for companionship.

PELFRIC RACIAL TRAITS

+2 Constitution, -2 Strength: Though lacking in physical strength, hey are hardy and surprisingly tough.

Medium-size: Pelfrics have no special bonuses or penalties due to their size. Pelfrics' base speed is 30 feet.

Automatic Language: Common. Bonus Languages: Dwarven, Goblin, and Orc.

Superior vision: Pelfrics receive a +2 racial bonus to all Spot and Search checks based on vision.

Favored Class: Bard. A multiclass pelfric's bard class does not count when determining whether he suffers an XP penalty. Easy-going and racially gifted with a knack for music and storytelling, pelfrics are often drawn to the bardic life.

TRUMMEL

Trummels are a close cousin to the zeetvah, and also originate in the Beast Mountain region. Trummels are largely unknown in the greater world but are universally disliked by those who do. They have a handful of small, filthy villages in the mid-region of the mountain range.

Personality: Trummels are born naturally greedy. If they see something they want, they cannot help but try to figure out a way to take it. Smaller and weaker than many other races, they have honed their stealth and thieving skills. Stealing is not regarded as a bad thing in trummel villages, as anyone worthy of an object will be able to take it (or get it back later). For a race of thieves, though, trummels are good-natured and try to make friends with others, and other races who know trummels realize that they are natural kleptomaniacs who will usually give an item back if challenged. Another common characteristic is a trummel's low intelligence and over-confidence. Trummels almost always believe they are smarter than they truly are, prompting them to say and do things that lead to danger.

Physical Description: Shorter than humans and elves, a trummel has a lean humanoid frame. Each trummel is covered with fuzzy hair, colors ranging from tan to dark brown. They have a short snout measured somewhere between that of a dog and cat, with two pronounced eye-teeth (usually dull and ineffective for biting). A trummel has large eyes (almost always brown or black, but rare specimens are found with light-colored eyes) and long ears—the latter curiously shaped like the long wings of a gull.

Relations: If they are an offshoot of the zeetvahs, the zeetvahs will not admit it. Trummels sometimes wander into the zeetvahs' valley and are politely but firmly escorted to the border. Trummels, working as individuals or in teams, have infiltrated the villages and homes of other races in the region, robbing people blind. Orcs and "mean" almeers will often attack a trummel on sight. Others will watch their valuables closely while one is nearby.

Alignment: Trummels are usually neutral in their moral outlook. They do not believe in hurting other people for the most part, but most possess a selfish worldview that makes them do things that are certainly not "lawful" or "good." Still, truly heinous acts are distasteful to them and they generally like to fancy themselves as "the good guys."

Religion: Most trummels do not spend much time pondering the existence of gods or greater powers, instead thinking about more earthly things—such as a neighbor's set of silver cutlery. Still, some trummels who manage to expand their horizons realize there may be greater forces at work, such as luck, darkness, and wealth. These should be respected, occasionally even worshipped—which led to the first trummel clerics, who remain rare to this day.

Language: It is unlikely for trummels to ever have had their own language other than the Common tongue they speak. A traveling trummel learns whatever language that is convenient for the journey. When speaking any language, most trummels do not bother to learn the more sophisticated pronunciations and longer words, instead speaking in broken, awkward sentences and using the smallest words possible.

Names: Being naturally lazy and not given to complicated thought, trummels have simple names of one- or two-syllables. They make no distinction among themselves between males and females, except during those special occasions that result in baby trummels.

Example: Barf, Jarp, Nelper, Sorb, Worpop.

Adventurers: Trummels are consistently motivated by greed. While many trummels are satisfied robbing each other, there are some who dream of something bigger. These ambitious trummels leave their home and venture out in search of "scores" truly worthy of a natural-born thief.

TRUMMEL RACIAL TRAITS

+2 Dexterity, -2 Constitution, -2 Strength: Inherently quick and agile, trummels are also often weak and frail when compared to humans.

Medium-size: Trummels have no special bonuses or penalties due to their size.

Trummels' base speed is 30 feet.

Automatic Language: Common. Bonus Languages: Dwarven, Elven, and Orc.

Natural stealth: Trummels receive a +2 racial bonus to Hide and Move Silently checks.

Favored Class: Rogue. A multiclass trummel's rogue class does not count when determining whether he suffers an XP penalty. Stealing is an expected part of a trummel's upbringing.

I think the key in having a very fun and humorous game is that your characters should not be very powerful, or at least have some weaknesses. Very powerful characters can solve problems too easily, this defeats the background "set up" work of the DM. If the heroes of SnarfQuest ran up against truly powerful characters, they would just avoid them with suspicions or simply run away.

ZEETVAH

Zeetvahs first appeared in their valley (nestled in the Beast Mountains) over two thousand years ago. The valley was rich in natural resources and food, and can be easily defended against attackers. While Zeetville is the largest town and seat of zeetvah government, there are several villages in the valley, as well as farm-families that live outside of the towns.

Personality: Zeetvahs seem to possess diverse personalities, much like humans. Most are hardworking folk, content with their lot in life, but others have ambition to better themselves or gain some power within the community. The trait that once defined zeetvahs was their love of their valley, and their reluctance to leave. With the ascension of Snarf as king of the valley, the younger generation has begun to hear more stories of the outside world. During Snarf's (often absentee) rule, there will be more zeetvahs roaming the greater world.

Physical Description: A zeetvah is shorter than a typical human, averaging about 4' 8" in height with a thin physique. Rarely have there been stout or even fat zeetvahs in the valley. Zeetvahs are generally stronger than they look, though they still lack the strength of larger races. A zeetvah is most easily identified by his snout, which is the longest of any humanoid race, and somewhat resembles an elephant's trunk, yet straight and aligned over its mouth (complete with fang-like teeth). Another universal trait is the long ears that resemble bat wings. A zeetvah's ears normally hang down but become animated by his action or emotion (such as when he is listening intently or is frightened out of his wits). Zeetvah skin is leathery to the touch, and is generally tan or light brown.

A zeetvah has a life-span comparable to a human's, though this can be shortened through disease, mischance, or adventure.

I'M SNARF'S BROTHER, FARF, THIS IS HIS FATHER, PARF, HIS SISTER, SWARF, AND HIS MAMMA, BERTHA.

G'DAY. HELLO. HI.

Relations: Zeetvahs rarely venture outside their valley, but small groups leave and explore each time they must crown a new king, making the zeetvahs known (if only by reputation) throughout the young lands, and bringing back stories of humans, elves, almeers, etc. The only regular contact they have are with trummels (who are kicked out of the valley regularly) and pelfrics (who occasionally wander through the area).

Alignment: Typical zeetvahs are neutral and good in alignment, working toward the general good of the community without being too strict in their laws. Most matters are settled among those involved, though greater issues are brought before the king—the final

arbiter of all laws and disagreements. Zeetvah rulers are usually more neutral in their alignment, as ambition and politics usually demand less scruples.

Religion: The zeetvahs feel that greater forces work in their world, and they consider themselves blessed by whatever gods responsible for their beautiful valley and (mostly) idyllic lifestyle. Clerics are rare among them, and are usually those who have picked up the such ideas from humans, dwarves, or elves in the outside world.

FINALLY THE VILLAGE ELDER SPOKE THREE WORDS...

SNARF IS KING!

THEN A ROAR WENT UP FROM THE CROWD THAT COULD BE HEARD FOR MILES.

Language: Zeetvahs have no language of their own, but instead have used Common since they began recording their history over one thousand years ago. The sophisticated zeetvahs from Zeetville are able to speak Common more elegantly. Those in the country have a crude vernacular that makes them sound less intelligent than they truly are.

Names: A zeetvah is given an individual name and has a last name for his family. While the names themselves vary widely, families often try to name their children with a similar theme, such as a rhyme-scheme or starting with the same letter. A zeetvah usually picks up one or more nicknames during his lifetime—either a shortened version of his name or something based on a famous (or infamous) incident in his life.

Adventurers: Zeetvahs are generally homebodies, preferring their safe and secure valley to the dangerous world outside. Usually the only zeetvah adventurers are candidates hoping to prove themselves worthy of the throne, as tradition dictates whichever champion comes back with the greatest wealth and tales of the most heroic deeds shall be declared king. When Snarf returned to Zeetville and claimed the throne, however, he inspired a new generation of zeetvahs to follow in his footsteps and venture out into the young lands.

ZEETVAH RACIAL TRAITS

+2 Dexterity, -2 Strength: Zeetvahs are often nimble and agile, but weaker than other races.

Medium-size: Zeetvahs have no special bonuses or penalties due to their size.

Zeetvahs' base speed is 30 feet.

Automatic Language: Common. Bonus Languages: Dwarven, Elven, Goblin, and Orc.

Superior hearing: Zeetvahs receive a +2 racial bonus to all Listen checks. Their large, flappy ears can hear very well.

Superior sense of smell: Zeetvahs receive a +2 racial bonus to Spot checks related to their sense of smell. Zeetvahs' noses are not as sensitive as some animals, but they can often smell when trouble is on the way.

Favored Class: Fighter. A multiclass zeetvah's fighter class does not count when determining whether he suffers an XP penalty. Generally peaceable folk, the zeetvahs nevertheless have been protecting their valley for centuries and have learned to defend themselves.

CHARACTER CLASSES

The traditional classes of the d20 System are all found in the old young lands, along with one more—the noble! Each class has a unique role in the setting, and some may vary slightly from the fantasy "norm." The normal d20 System rules for acquiring classes and multiclassing apply in the world of SnarfQuest.

SNARF POSED FOR AN OFFICIAL PORTRAIT TO BE HUNG IN THE HALL OF HEROES IN THE CASTLE OF QUESSA.

BARBARIAN

More of an attitude and fighting style than a declaration of culture and heritage, the barbarian class represents warriors who favor force over finesse, power over technique. Many barbarians do come from primitive cultures (such as the "mean" almeers), but there are also those who simply dedicate themselves to bloody combat.

Character Creation: Being a barbarian is about being angry. Someone, somewhere, has done you wrong and one day they're gonna pay. If someone hasn't done you wrong yet, they will eventually. Until then, you'll make every jerk sorry for getting in your way. Figure out just what your barbarian is so angry about, then make your character as normal.

BARD

The bard is a rare profession in the young lands, though not unheard of. As cities grow and men explore more of the wilds, the need for traveling news, stories, and songs becomes greater each year. Bards do all of this and more, all the while picking up bits of lore and learning a touch of magic from local spellcasters. As singing for dinner does not work every time, most bards also pick up a few less popular skills in order to keep them in gold and food during their journeys. Charismatic and artistic, many bards seem to have a way with the ladies, though most minstrels do not wish to be saddled with a permanent girlfriend or wife.

Character Creation: Give your bard some motivation. Is he an artist ahead of his time, pursuing avant-garde music or poetry that may never be accepted by the common folk? Is he more of a stand-up comedian, spreading news and jokes alongside his unflattering impressions of the local sheriff? Or perhaps he is just a con artist, looking to trade his passable bardic talent for free beer and a room at the local inn?

CLERIC

In this young land, a formal pantheon of deities has not been established yet, and every race (and major city, for that matter) has its own take on the gods, the creation of the world, and the nature of higher powers. The ones who have the strongest debates on this subject are the clerics, except that you can't get more than a handful to agree. Some have names, histories, and pictures of their gods, while others simply revere abstract "powers" and believe there are no true gods but simply pure good, evil, light, truth, etc. Other belief systems lead the search for powers in bizarre places. (The Mushroom Cult, for example, insists the divine can be found in the study, reverence, and consumption of 'shrooms.)

Character Creation: Clerics are created as usual, except that the gods presented in Core Rulebook I have no presence in the young lands (unless you want them to be "made up" by your cleric's limited following). Choose your domains as you wish, and feel free to have a truly bizarre mystery cult as the basis of your cleric's religion—including weird oaths, strange practices, and odd garb to round out your cleric. (Humor is the aim here, don't be shy. If a religion based on goats being divine presences and every cleric must take one with him on adventure is what you want, go ahead and put it in.)

DRUID

Druids are like clerics, except they believe that divinity exists in nature, not in some distant "gods" whose existence is debatable. The power of nature is real, but there are definite rules for harnessing it. Some druids tie their powers to the sea, and can only renew their spells during high tide. Others are druids of the moon, who only meditate on their magic during a full moon. More stable, but limited, are the druids of the stones; they are able to renew and use their powers anytime, but must do so within a druidic stone circle. Of course, requiring a Druid to carry fresh manure in his pockets at all time as a component of all his spells might lead to some, uh, funny occasions. Particularly in areas where the inhabitants might be somewhat more olfactorially aware.

Character Creation: You must choose a type for your druid in SnarfQuest: Druid of the Sea, Druid of the Moon, or Druid of the Stones. (You may invent another designation with

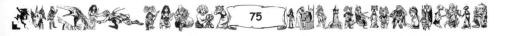

DM's permission.) Attempting to overcome the limitations of druidic spell renewal can be an adventure all by itself! And Druids whose power is tied to a particularly desolate spot could spark some humor… Druid of the Sink Holes, for instance.

HEH, HEH!

FIGHTER

The trusty fighter is not much changed in the young lands. A soldier, sell-sword, gladiator, or wandering warrior, a fighter can be of any race or background. Since magic is a bit more rare in the world of SnarfQuest, there are more characters in the fighter class than any other.

Character Creation: Congratulations! You picked a class that doesn't complicate character creation. Just match your feat and skill choices with a background suitable for a fighter.

MONK

Lin-Yu's family sent him to learn from the master, high up in the mountains. For an entire year, the master made Lin-Yu do nothing but fill a basin with water, and then slap at the water until the basin was empty. Once the water was gone, Lin-Yu had to re-fill the basin and repeat the process. All day, every day, for one year. When allowed to return home for a visit with his family, they all gathered around him, eager to find out just what amazing combat skills Lin-Yu had learned in a year's time. Frustrated, Lin-Yu shouted, "In truth, I have learned nothing!" and angrily slammed his fist down on the family's table. Lin-Yu looked down in surprise. The force of the blow had snapped the table in two. His family then knew that the tales of the monks' skills were no mere legend.

—*Excerpt taken from Tales of Lin-Yu, Slayer of Water Elementals, page 22.*

Character Creation: Your character comes from a land in the far east, but has had the fundamental training in a discipline of powerful martial arts. The ways of the westerners are strange to you, just as your ways and appearance seem bizarre to others. Alternatively, you are a young lands character who has met and studied under one of the rare masters who has journeyed into the heart of the Beast Mountains. These masters will accept anyone willing to study in humility and honor the ancient ways. Remember, your character must live a lifestyle that supports his amazing physical abilities. Diet, breathing, meditation, and philosophy are all a part of this. Start saving the proverbs from fortune cookies—they make excellent quotes in monk dialogue. Naturally, anything said while planting your foot in someone's face can be funny.

NOBLE

Most cultures have a clear division between commoners and the aristocracy. Wealth, education, power, and privilege are available to those born into noble or royal families. Along with these benefits come the responsibilities and duties of title and rank.

Nobles can often be identified by wealth and its trappings. Early in a noble's career, he begins acquiring cohorts and followers to do his bidding—more so than other classes. A noble generally dresses in the finest clothes, drinks the finest wines, and surrounds himself with the luxuries only a selected few can afford. The noble has a surprising balance to his skills. He is trained with weapons and armor, both to lead those under his rule into battle and to defend himself and his family's honor in a duel. The noble also understands the sometimes dangerous games of intrigue played in the royal courts, and is knowledgeable in the subtle arts of information-gathering, blackmail, and character assassination.

Nobles are often found among humans, elves, and dwarves. Some of the other races do not have the social divisions to produce a noble character.

Game Rule Information

Abilities: Since the noble's skills cover a wide variety of disciplines, an individual could do well by focusing on any one ability. It is important to remember that in the arenas of politics and intrigue, Charisma and Wisdom serve the noble best.

Restrictions: The noble must be a character's starting class. If another class is selected at first level, the player cannot choose noble as a multiclass option (although a noble may later multiclass into any other available class). Also, while the player is free to choose a character's starting race and class, the referee is the final authority on the exact title and position of the new character. The player and referee should work together to create an appropriate background.

Hit Die: d8.

Class Skills

The noble's class skills (and the key ability for each skill) are Appraise (Int), Bluff (Cha), Diplomacy (Cha), Disguise (Cha), Forgery (Int), Gather Information (Cha), Handle Animal (Cha), Innuendo (Wis), Intimidate (Cha), Knowledge (all skills taken individually) (Int), Listen (Wis), Perform (Cha), Read Lips (Int, exclusive skill), Ride (Dex), Sense Motive (Wis), Speak Language, Spot (Wis), Swim (Str), and Wilderness Lore (Wis).

Class Features

Weapon and Armor Proficiency: The noble is proficient in the use of all simple and martial weapons and with all types of armor and shields. Note that heavy armor results in a negative modifier for certain Dexterity-based skills.

TABLE: THE NOBLE

Level	Base Attack Bonus	Fort Save	Ref Save	Will Save	Special
1	+0	+0	+0	+2	Deceptive Melee
2	+1	+0	+0	+3	Available Funds (25gp)
3	+2	+1	+1	+3	
4	+3	+1	+1	+4	
5	+3	+1	+1	+4	
6	+4	+2	+2	+5	Leadership Feat
7	+5	+2	+2	+5	
8	+6/+1	+2	+2	+6	Available Funds (50gp)
9	+6/+1	+3	+3	+6	
10	+7/+2	+3	+3	+7	Leadership +1
11	+8/+3	+3	+3	+7	Available Funds (100gp)
12	+9/+4	+4	+4	+8	Silver Tongue
13	+9/+4	+4	+4	+8	
14	+10/+5	+4	+4	+9	
15	+11/+6/+1	+5	+5	+9	Leadership +2
16	+12/+7/+2	+5	+5	+10	
17	+12/+7/+2	+5	+5	+10	Available Funds (200gp)
18	+13/+8/+3	+6	+6	+11	
19	+14/+9/+4	+6	+6	+11	
20	+15/+10/+5	+6	+6	+12	Leadership +3

Talent for Intrigue: The noble's knowledge of gossip, rumor, and politics gives him a +2 competence bonus to Bluff, Innuendo, and Sense Motive skills checks.

Deceptive Melee: At 1st level a noble knows how to use feints and goading to evade opponents while fighting unarmored. He may add his Charisma bonus to his AC in addition to his Dexterity bonus. If the noble dons armor—even padded—he is too encumbered to use these techniques. At 8th level the noble may use these techniques while wearing light armor. At 17th level the noble may use the Deceptive Melee ability in medium (or lighter) armor.

Available Funds: Beginning at 2nd level, the noble starts receiving monthly sums of money either from banked wealth or as an allowance from his estate. The noble can receive 25 gold pieces each month at 2nd level, 50 gold pieces at 8th level, 100 gold pieces at 11th level, and 200 gold pieces at 17th level and higher. The funds are available only in the noble's native land (or at DM's discretion) and are in addition to any wealth the character has accumulated through adventuring.

Leadership: A noble is born into a leadership position and is trained to lead from a very early age. At 6th level the noble receives the leadership feat for free. At 10th level he receives a +1 bonus to his leadership score. At 15th level the bonus is increased to +2. The noble's leadership score receives a +3 bonus at 20th level. This enables the noble to recruit more followers (of higher level) than other character classes of the same level. The followers become loyal retainers to the noble's family and are usually available if he calls upon them for aid.

Silver Tongue: At 12th level the noble can attempt to win trust and favor by using flattery and charm. To do so, the noble rolls a Bluff check. The noble's target must make a Will save against a DC equal to the noble's Bluff check. If the saving throw is not successful, the individual regards the noble as a trusted ally or friend and will heed most reasonable suggestions his "friend" proposes. If the noble abuses this friendship by advising a dangerous course of action, the target may make a Will save against a DC 10 + noble's level to come to his senses. This ability to influence will fade after a week's time, although the target's opinion of the noble will remain high. If the noble wishes to make other suggestions after this time has elapsed, he must make another Bluff check, allowing the target a saving throw as normal. However, unless something has occurred to change the target's opinion of the noble, his saving throw is at –2.

PALADIN

In a world in which the gods are not clearly defined and agreed upon by the mortal populace, holy warriors are quite rare. But they do exist—usually from large kingdoms and city-states where there are established churches or temples. Along with the clergy there are champions—the paladins—who serve their god and the priesthood, looking to slay evil, right wrongs, and do good where it needs doing. It's too bad that people like this just aren't appreciated everywhere.

Character Creation: Becoming a holy champion is something that takes dedication, devotion, and (let's face it) arrogance. The greater world doesn't appreciate your efforts, but so what? Your god has defined right and wrong, and if this doesn't match with what the local guard captain says, so be it! Do you think he's going to stop you? Other people don't always know what's for their own good, either. Good thing you're around to show them. Create your character as normal, just make sure you got the right attitude for your paladin in a SnarfQuest campaign.

RANGER

The world of SnarfQuest is the world of the young lands—a primitive, primal environment where most areas have not been explored, most trails unblazed, and the Average Joes don't travel past twenty miles in their entire lives. Not so the ranger. He is a man of the wilderness, marking maps, identifying game trails, exploring the continent far past any known borders. Rangers tend to encroach on the territory of other races, animals, and monsters, so they do make enemies. That's okay, because the rangers study their enemies and learn how to fight them effectively. There are usually one or two creatures that rangers absolutely hate. No mercy shown there. If a ranger so much as spots one of his nemesis, he will stop at nothing to slay it, scalp it, and leave its carcass for the vultures.

Character Creation: Going off into the wilderness and being a ranger are two different things. Your character actually likes sleeping under the stars, on the ground, in the cold, and doesn't seem to mind poison ivy, bug bites, or boot blisters. Pick your chosen enemy seriously, as these things set you off every time you see them. Invent a reason why you're so hot to kill your nemesis race.

ROGUE

The d20 System is rather kind in letting these guys slide with the moniker of "rogue." It sounds kind of romantic, doesn't it? Reality check: You are a thief. All those points and you're not going to take skills that let you slink around in the dark, pick those pockets, open those locks, disarm those pesky treasure-chest traps? A rogue's abilities are geared toward stealth, getting the hell out of the way of danger, and striking an enemy only when his back is turned. Hmm, that does sounds cool...

Character Creation: Embrace the idea your rogue is a thief! You wouldn't have taken this class if you weren't looking out for Number One, right? (And we're not talking about the guy with three pips on his collar.) Create your "rogue" as normal, but establish behavior and motives early on, as well as style. Are you a lowly cut-purse, or a safe-cracking second-story thief? Do you con people out of their money with words, or do you prefer riskier methods such as you and ten of your closest friends gang-rolling a little old lady coming home from a night of winning bingo? It's all up to you, "thief," but remember that when you do the crime, you might have to do some time (assuming they don't just cut your hands off).

SORCERER

For some, magic comes through exacting, excruciating study, requiring repetitive exercises to learn the same spells over and over. Too bad for them, for sorcerers learn magic quickly and easily. Sorcerers do not need to prepare spells in advance; they simply channel their magical energy into whatever spell they need at the time. Of course, as with anything, there's a catch. Sorcerers have extremely limited repertoires. Lesser sorcerers are one-trick ponies, while some actually manage to learn a few new spells.

Character Creation: The magic of sorcery and wizardry is the same power, used in two completely different ways. Both require a certain amount of discipline to gain the basic levels of mastery. A 1st-level sorcerer has passed this "apprenticeship" phase and can now cast spells. He will figure new ones out as he progresses in level. Wizards who train sorcerers are first frustrated by how easy the first few spells seem to their proteges, then snicker when they realize these sorcerers will never master more than a few spells at each level of power. Figure out where your character achieved magical knowledge, then create your character normally.

> A tip about magic: don't let your wizards get too powerful. As they grow in power the DM should keep them in check by creating problems so that every spell doesn't go off as expected. The magic user could slip and fall at the most critical time when casting a spell, or the spell comes off too good and does too much damage. Again, in real life things usually don't go exactly as planned.

WIZARD

A wizard has huge spellbooks with hundreds of pages, including recipes for spells beyond a sorcerer's wildest dreams. True mastery of magic requires study and preparation. Sorcerers quickly find out that their limited range does not meet the situation, while a wizard can anticipate the situation and prepare appropriate spells for that day. A wizard who studies under a sorcerer at first flummoxes his master with his need to write everything down, then surpasses the master with his repertoire of spells.

Character Creation: Decide where your character received magical training, as the 1st-level period is just after an apprenticeship. Masters sometimes make demands of their former students, or develop resentment when the baby bird leaves the "nest."

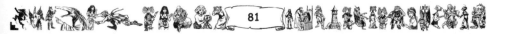

PRESTIGE CLASSES

The full range of d20 System prestige classes are available in the world of SnarfQuest, though the DM is encouraged to find a "hook" to make the class fit the tone and style of the setting. A new prestige class is available as well and presented below.

KNIGHT OF THE ORDER OF ROBOT

"I'm a Robot, I never wed.
I'm a Robot, I'm seldom fed.
I'm a Robot, I hardly sleep.
I'm a Robot, I go Bleep."

—*The catechism of the Knights of the Order of Robot*

The bards still sing of the day Saint Aveeare liberated the city-state of Quessa from the evil wizard Suthaze and the wrath of his terrible red dragon. Princess Penelope, daughter of the king, offered herself in marriage to St. Aveeare, but his dedication to his cause was so great, he could not return her affections. However, he taught her the precepts of the Order, so that his ways could propagate throughout the young lands. Princess Penelope gave up parties, wine, food, and fashionable clothes, and began teaching others the ways of the Order. She hopes that one day, her true love will return.

A Knight of the Order of Robot (now the only recognized knighthood in Quessa) performs heroic deeds and will quest far to assist those in need, just as St. Aveeare journeyed far to rescue the city of Quessa. He wears armor in the image of the founder and usually has a lance painted a bright red. In order to be pure, a knight gives up most comforts:

A knight will remain in armor for as long as possible, long after he has become sore and weary.

A knight will forever give up the companionship of the opposite sex and will never marry. (This means "grown up" companionship, boys and girls. Knights are allowed to socialize with the opposite sex, as long as things don't go too far.)

A knight will not eat until hunger has forced him to pass out at least once.

A knight will not sleep until exhaustion causes him to collapse.

The knights understand they are on a long road to reach the perfection of St. Aveeare, and may never truly reach the Revered One's level. St. Aveeare, it is said, never slept, never ate, never removed his armor, and did not show the slightest discomfort. The Order also realizes the rest of the world regards them with confusion and pity, not realizing they are striving for great things, in the name of the First Robot.

Hit Die: 1d8

Requirements

To qualify to become a Knight of the Order of Robot, a character must fulfill all the following criteria:

Alignment: Lawful Good or Lawful Neutral.

Base Attack Bonus: +4.

Ride: 4 ranks.

Knowledge (History): 4 ranks.

Feats: Endurance, Iron Will.

Special: The knight must have made a pilgrimage to the Tower of Robot in Quessa and seek an audience with Penelope. Only if deemed worthy can anyone become a Knight of Robot.

TABLE: THE KNIGHT OF THE ORDER OF ROBOT

Level	Base Attack Bonus	Fort Save	Ref Save	Will Save	Special
1	+1	+2	+0	+2	Granted Armor, Sleep Resistance
2	+2	+3	+0	+3	Great Endurance
3	+3	+3	+1	+3	
4	+4	+4	+1	+4	Hunger Resistance
5	+5	+4	+1	+4	Improved Sleep Resistance
6	+6	+5	+2	+5	
7	+7	+5	+2	+5	Determination
8	+8	+6	+2	+6	Improved Great Endurance
9	+9	+6	+3	+6	
10	+10	+7	+3	+7	Improved Determination, Granted Magical Weapon

Class Skills: A Knight of the Order of Robot's class skills (and key abilities for each skill) are Craft (Int), Diplomacy (Cha), Handle Animal (Cha), Knowledge (History), Intuit Direction (Wis), and Ride (Dex).

Skill Points at Each Level: 2 + Int modifier.

Class Features

All of the following are class features for the Knight of the Order of Robot prestige class.
Weapon and Armor Proficiency: Knights are proficient with all simple and martial weapons, with all types of armor, and shields.

Granted Armor: Upon acceptance into the order, a Knight of the Order of Robot is given a special, custom-designed suit of full plate armor, made in the image of St. Aveeare.
Sleep Resistance: A Knight of the Order of Robot has learned to fight fatigue and the need for sleep. He can go twice as long as a normal member of his race without rest. He also gains a +4 circumstance bonus to saving throws versus sleep effects.
Great Endurance: The bonus granted by the Endurance feat doubles, becoming +8.
Hunger Resistance: A Knight of the Order of Robot has learned to push his body farther without nourishment. He can go twice as long as a normal member of his race without food. He also gains a +4 circumstance bonus to saving throws versus any magical effects that induce hunger.

Determination: A Knight of the Order of Robot develops single-minded dedication to his assigned mission (either dictated or approved by Penelope). When performing tasks that directly contribute to completing his given mission, he receives a +2 circumstance bonus (to attack rolls, ability checks, skill checks, and saving throws). The DM has final authority on what directly contributes to the mission.

Improved Great Endurance: The bonus granted by the Endurance feat is tripled, becoming +12.

Improved Determination: The bonus granted by Determination doubles, becoming +4.

Granted Magical Weapon: Upon achieving the pinnacle of knighthood, the Knight is granted a magical weapon by Penelope. The item is determined by the DM and is between 5,000 and 10,000 gp in value—often a magical sword or lance, but occasionally an enchanted item that shoots magical energy, much like the fabled "lasers" of St. Aveeare.

Ex-Knights

If a Knight ever leaves the order or begins living a "normal" life (eating, drinking, and resting regularly), the benefits of his hard life begin to leave him. For each month after leaving the order, an ex-Knight will lose one special benefit of the prestige class, from highest level to lowest. (Granted magical items and armor do not go away, obviously, only insubstantial benefits.)

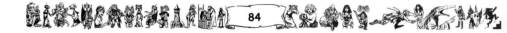

NEW SKILL

There are always new things to learn, and in the old young lands it's not so easy to learn to read as in other d20 System settings. Many people go their entire lives without learning to read more than a few letters and put an "X" mark to sign their name.

LITERACY (NONE; TRAINED ONLY)

In the lands of SnarfQuest, the ability to speak a language does not mean you are able to read and write it. Literacy permits a character to read and write one of the languages he speaks.

At 1st level, you may decide to use Intelligence bonus points to become literate in a language that you already know how to speak.

Instead of buying a rank in Literacy, you choose a new language to read and write (so long as you already speak the chosen language).

You do not need to make Literacy checks. Those literate in a language are able to read and write without fear of failure.

It is possible for a language to not have written alphabets and therefore cannot be written or read.

Retry: Not applicable. (There are no Literacy checks to fail.)

NEW FEATS

There are several new tricks your character can acquire in the world of SnarfQuest, from combat options to an increased dose of luck.

Table: New Feats

Feat	Pre-requisite
Dead Shot	Point Blank Shot, Precise Shot, Dex 13+, base attack +4
Improved Mounted Combat	Mounted Combat Feat, Dex 13+, Ride skill 6 ranks
Improvised Weapon	Base attack bonus +4
Fortune's Fool	None
Subduing Strike	Dex 13+, base attack bonus +2 or higher

DEAD SHOT [GENERAL]

You are a skilled marksman and have learned to hit targets who are hiding behind cover.

Prerequisites: Point Blank Shot, Precise Shot, Dex 13+, base attack bonus +4 or higher.

Benefit: When firing a heavy crossbow, light crossbow, longbow (normal or composite), or shortbow (normal or composite) at a target taking advantage of cover, the target is considered at one less cover category. For example, a target behind three-quarters cover normally receives a +7 AC bonus and a +3 Reflex save bonus. A Dead-Shot target in a similar situation would receive the bonuses for just one-half cover (+4 AC bonus/+2 Reflex save bonus) instead. (See Core Rulebook I, page 133, for the full effects of cover.)

Special: This feat does not stack with other feats or abilities that lend modifiers to hit targets behind cover.

IMPROVED MOUNTED COMBAT [GENERAL]

You have mastered the art of mounted combat and are able to effectively protect your mount in battle.

Prerequisites: Mounted Combat Feat, Dex 13+, Ride skill 6+.

Benefit: Your mount receives a +2 bonus to its AC and Reflex saving throws. In addition, you may make a Ride check to negate an amount of damage to your mount equal to your Dexterity bonus.

Special: A mounted warrior gains this feat automatically at 8th level, regardless of pre-requisites.

IMPROVISED WEAPON [GENERAL]

You are adept at grabbing any small object within reach and using it as an effective weapon.

Prerequisites: Base attack bonus +4 or greater.

Benefit: You may use any small, hard object as a weapon (at DM's discretion) that inflicts 1d4 points of damage. Type of damage (bludgeoning, slashing, or piercing) is determined by the DM. You may apply your base attack bonus and Strength bonus to the improvised weapon, but not benefits from feats (such as Weapon Focus).

FORTUNE'S FOOL [GENERAL]

You have greater extremes of luck than most people, both good and bad.

Prerequisites: None

Benefit: A "natural" roll of 19 or 20 is always a success (usually a surprising success with unforeseen positive consequences) on any attack, skill check, ability check, or saving throw. Conversely, a natural roll of 1 or 2 is always a failure—even if the modified result would normally be a success. Note that this does not increase a weapon's critical threat range, just the numbers necessary for an automatic hit or miss.

Normal: Without this feat, a roll of 20 is always a success and a 1 is always a failure.

Special: You may only take this feat as a 1st level character.

SUBDUING STRIKE [GENERAL]

You've learned how to knock your opponents unconscious with lethal weapons.

Prerequisites: Dex 13+, base attack bonus +2 or higher.

Benefit: When using a normal weapon to inflict only subdual damage, the normal –4 attack penalty is reduced to –2.

Special: This feat may be taken twice to reduce the modifier for subdual attacks to –0. You cannot take this feat more than twice.

Chapter 4:
Magic and Tech

During Snarf's many adventures, magic and technology constantly affected his life. The first friend he met was a magically altered human prince, then he ran afoul of an evil wizard, a spellstruck dragon, and liberated a bag full of magic wands. Time travel brought technology to a world unready for it—both by the time-jumping wizard Suthaze and accidentally by the robot Aveeare. By the end of his adventures, Snarf has acquired several pieces of magic and technology for himself, including a magical backpack and a 20th century revolver! Snarf eventually returns home to Zeetville in a flying spaceship capable of time-travel and faster-than-light speed.

ARCANE MAGIC

The magic of wizards and sorcerers is rare enough in the old young lands that most towns do not have an arcane spellcaster in residence. If someone has talent or desire to learn magic, they either have pursue magical research on their own (a dangerous choice, and one that takes a great deal of time), or they must leave and find an experienced teacher.

There are occasional "hedge-wizards" who set up shop here and there, but the truly powerful arcane spellcasters seem to live in more remote locations: towers, keeps, or remote sites in the wilderness. Some live in total isolation, pursuing magical research or enchanting magical objects, while others build a stronghold complete with minions, guards, and magically dominated creatures.

Magical power seems to augment the more obsessive traits in many arcane spellcasters. Gathgor became consumed with accumulating riches, Suthaze with time-travel, and Etheah with "fighting evil." Such people quickly become out of touch with the outside world (and common sense). When their magical toys are taken away from them, they react badly. (Etheah wandered off into the woods, crying, after her wand was taken. Suthaze flew into a berserk rage when Geezel broke the hourglass of time-jumping.)

While the "rules" of arcane magic are the same in SnarfQuest as presented in the d20 System, both players and the DM should understand the tone and role-play characters appropriately.

DIVINE MAGIC

The old young lands are a place in which the gods have not exactly sorted themselves out into an identifiable pantheon. Some men will tell you there are no gods, and that clerics are simply a different type of wizard—using talk of "divine beings" and "faith" to dupe the gullible into filling the cleric's coffers with gold. Other people follow a highly organized religion, complete with religious rituals, holidays, rites, and ceremonies—convinced that their religion is correct and the truly faithful will be rewarded in the next life. The average person takes the middle ground: there are probably gods, but they are distant and hard to understand. So why try?

Clerics and druids, of course, believe that their powers come from truly divine sources, the gods or Mother Earth herself. Whether they are correct is the subject for scholarly debate. Regardless, such faith is rewarded by someone or something in the form of divine magic. The belief system is self-fulfilling. If a mushroom cleric believes he can only replenish his spells by consuming hallucinogenic mushrooms, it becomes true. If another faith demands that the priest pray for his magic while dunking his head in a bucket of water, this is true for him.

Such men and women easily become zealous. They are granted divine power, after all, so they feel it is their moral duty to push their beliefs on others. The mushroom cleric might slip toadstools into his comrades' food, in order for them to also experience the glory of the Shroom God. They are often patient and gracious with a potential "flock," trying to win them over with kindness and not-so-gentle nudging. They reserve contempt and hatred for the clerics of other faiths. When you have two people of different faiths, each granted power, they will butt heads and constantly argue. Even if the situation demands they cooperate, they cannot resist the chance to make subtle digs at each other's religion.

The rules for divine magic are the same as the core d20 System, except that the gods found in Core Rulebook I are not part of the young lands. The DM should work with the player in creating a clerical faith. A cleric may be a lone maverick attempting to build a new church, or a young priest following a long-established religion. Such faiths should have restrictions on the manner and time a cleric may renew spells—much in the same way druids have increased restrictions (see Chapter One).

PSIONICS IN SNARFQUEST

The power of the mind has not been specifically shown in the world of SnarfQuest, but that certainly does not mean it is absent! Such power would be extremely rare— encountered far less than arcane and divine magic.

In SnarfQuest, people with supernatural powers are not normal. (And whether many people in this world are "normal" is arguable, anyway.) Anyone who has tapped into the inner potential of his mind has bound to have fried a few brain cells along the way. A psionic character might become occasionally crossed-eyed, develop a nervous tick, or start speaking backwards. They could very well be slightly schizophrenic, a bit paranoid, and could have difficulty relating to others.

Psychic power could also make such a character feel more intelligent and powerful than those around him, a personality that certainly would irritate the rest of the world. This might make for an interesting player character but also has great potential as a villain—a "wizard" with powers far different than the party has encountered.

If you want to use psionics in SnarfQuest, by all means go ahead—just stay true to the spirit of the setting and have fun with it!

NEW SPELL

IDENTITY CRISIS
Enchantment (Compulsion) [Mind-Affecting]
Level: Brd 5, Sor/Wiz 5
Components: V, S, XP
Casting Time: 1 round
Range: Close (25 ft. + 5 ft./2 levels)
Target: One creature
Duration: 1 week/level
Saving Throw: Will negates
Spell Resistance: Yes

Causes a designated creature to believe it is a completely different type of creature. Identity Crisis can be cast on any staggered or unconscious creature. The spell has no effect if cast upon a conscious creature with 1 or more hit points. The caster chooses a type of creature during the casting of the spell. If the target fails its saving throw, it will believe it is the specified type of creature, behaving and responding in precise manners as the creature specified. It also ignores any obvious physical disparities; for example, if an orc was compelled to believe he was a hamster, he could look in a mirror and believe he is seeing a tiny hamster. The target's abilities, skills, and special characteristics do not change—only his perception of himself. The target does not gain any extra special abilities or qualities.

The spell requires a trigger that will end the spell early. This is always the name of the target's original creature type. In the above example, if someone were to shout "orc" at the target, the spell would cease immediately and the orc would now behave like an orc again. Once the spell ends, the target has full memory of what happened while under its effect. XP Cost: 200 XP.

TECHNOLOGICAL & MAGICAL ITEMS

Listed below are items that Snarf and his companions encountered in The old young lands during the first year of Snarf's adventuring. It demonstrates the wide variety of enchanted and anachronistic items that can be found in the young lands.

Just about any magical item listed in the Core Rulebook II is appropriate for the world of SnarfQuest. Many magical items may just be small variations from what is found, while others could be unique and specific to the world.

Anachronistic technological devices, from the 20th century or further in the future, tend to find their way into The old young lands too. Suthaze is only one of three time-jumping wizards in the world, and Aveeare and Fred cannot be the only time-travelers from the future to visit the young lands. Many tech items have limitations to restrict their uses. A motorcycle only has so much gasoline, a revolver has only six bullets, a flashlight uses batteries, etc.

BIKINI ARMOR (the WOW factor)

As mentioned elsewhere, people in the SnarfQuest world (expecially women) are, mostly, all beautiful. Couple this fact with the soaring cost of armor, the flexability needed to dodge wizardly bolts, the advantages of a lighter weight armor, or to accomplish a Snarf's special 'Rear Advance' (elsewhere know as the retreat), Bikini armor is ones most logical choice.

This fantastic advance in armor technology is not limited to only females, or to those deemed 'attractive'. No, this type of armor works equally well when worn by the beautiful Telerie or the not-so-beautiful Snarf himself. Imagine the difficulty of trying to fight an opponent showing more skin than you care to see, such as Dorque the Wanderer wearing a thong!

Cost: 100gp; *Max Dex Bonus:* +4; *ACP*: 0; *ASF*: 10%; 30ft 20ft 15lb; Takes as long to get on as studded leather. *Armor Bonus:* Any character wearing Bikini Armor gains a +1 distraction bonus for each +/-1 Charisma Modifier; therefore a character with a 10 Charisma will have a +0AC, BUT characters with a Chaisma of 18 or 2 will have a +4AC.

I like to mix technology and magic. When Snarf uses his pistol, in his world, it is truly a magical feat! When Aveeare or anyone from a technology based world witness's real magic, it blows their mind because they do not believe in magic. Give a character in Snarf's world a few bits of technology or a unique tool, even a cigarette lighter, and they could become a great wizard. Give someone in the modern world a little magic and he can become powerful. Mix the two and you get craziness! All this can lead to a lot of laughs.

BELT PACK OF HOLDING (Wondrous Item)

After returning the wand of wishing to Etheah of the Woodland, she gave Snarf a magical pack, one that would hold as much as a large trunk without getting heavy. Snarf used it from that day forward, storing all of his supplies and many of his treasures without slowing him down.

DAT'S JUS' INCREDIBLE.

The belt pack appears to be a small, standard leather belt pouch. It opens into a nondimensional space. Regardless of what is put into the bag, its weight remains 15 lbs. The pack can hold up to 250 lbs. and a total volume of 30 cubic feet.

If the belt pack is overloaded or pierced by a sharp object (from inside or out), it ruptures and all contents are lost forever. If a living, breathing creature is placed within the bag (and it is closed) they will begin to suffocate after 10 minutes. Mixing the belt pack with other extradimensional objects is extremely dangerous and will certainly destroy the items (see Core Rulebook II, Chapter 8, Bag of Holding for more details).

Caster Level: 9th. *Prerequisites:* Craft Wondrous Item, *Leomund's Secret Chest. Market price:* 2,500 gp.

HORSE MACHINE

A.K.A. "MOTORCYCLE" (Technological Item)

Suthaze was riding the "horse machine" when he returned from his last time-jump. He told Geezel that "a lot of people drive them and dress like this. It's a blast!" Indeed, there was a blast shortly afterwards which destroyed the horse machine (and Suthaze's Tower). It's possible, however, that another horse machine could be recovered from the future...

THIS RE-ENTRY BUSINESS IS GONNA KILL ME... I GOTTA GET MY TIMING RIGHT!

This futuristic vehicle can move up to 1,200 feet per round on flat terrain (though it must accelerate up to that speed the previous round). Without the flat, hard roads it was designed for, the horse machine runs at a far less speed (DM's discretion). It will operate for six continuous hours before needing gasoline, and after three months of use requires maintenance, oil, spare parts, and other things not found in the young lands. It has a Hardness of 5 and 20 hit points.

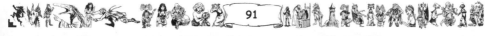

Riding the horse machine is easy enough to learn, though maneuvering can be tricky. Dexterity checks are required to negotiate obstacles. The DC is predicated on speed, visibility, and other conditions. In a crash, both the horse machine and rider will suffer 1d6 points of damage for every 30 feet of speed per round they were traveling, to a maximum of 20d6. If the horse machine is completely destroyed (losing all hit points), its fuel tank ruptures with a 50% chance of explosion that is equivalent to a fireball cast by a 6th level wizard, centered on the machine.

HOURGLASS OF TIME-JUMPING
(Major Magical Artifact)
The hourglass of time-jumping was the rare magical tool used by Suthaze to travel into the future. It is one of only a handful of time-travel devices in the entire world. The hourglass was accidentally destroyed by Geezel, forcing Suthaze to look for other means to acquire futuristic technology.

The hourglass lets one creature travel forward in time for up to 1,000 years per character level. The user may also choose a destination (as teleport without error). Once 72 hours has elapsed, the hourglass will bring the user back exactly to the point in both time and space he started at, along with anything he is in direct physical contact with (up to Large size). The time spent in the future matches the time the user is gone in the present.

ONE-SHOT WISH RING (Magical Ring)

I is not a real good poet,
But I have brains enough to know it.
I'm just a little magic man,
I forged this ring with my own hand.

And yes, I know this ring be small,
It's still the grandest gift of all.
Be ye fowl or be ye fish,
It don't matter, ye gots a wish!

—Enscribed Upon the Ring

Snarf thought he was giving the leech a relatively worthless ring, but instead gave away some potent magical power. The leech used this to gain its telepathic communications power, which would later have great repercussions for Snarf and the rest of the world.

No one knows exactly who made these rings, but every few years another turns up in some treasure pile or jewelry box. The "magic man" mentioned in the poem must enjoy distributing wishes randomly. Somewhere he probably watches the wishers, highly amused at the consequences.

A one-shot wish ring always resembles a cheap piece of jewelry, with the poem engraved on the band in tiny letters revealed only with extremely close inspection. It otherwise is identical to a ring of three wishes with only one wish.

SNARF'S PISTOL, A.K.A. "REVOLVER"
(Technological Item)

Originally a "magic weapon" that Suthaze brought back from the future, it was stolen by Geezel who quickly lost it to Snarf. The zeetvah then later slew a terrible dragon with it to save Zeetville, securing his claim to the throne.

The trained use of the pistol requires the Exotic Weapon Proficiency (Pistol) feat. Damage 2d6; Critical 19-20/x3; Range Increment 30 ft.; Weight 2 lbs.; Type P. The revolver holds six rounds before it must be reloaded.

WAND OF LIGHT, A.K.A. "FLASHLIGHT"
(Technological Item)

Brought back from the future from one of Suthaze's many time-jumps, the wand of light was liberated by Snarf before the destruction of Suthaze's tower. It then became part of his standard equipment, occasionally using it when it was dark and at least once shining it in the eyes of an enemy as a distraction.

The wand of light illuminates up to 30 feet, though its beam is a narrow cone just 10 feet in diameter at full range. If shined in someone's eyes, the target must make a Reflex saving throw (DC 8) or become dazzled for 1d4 rounds.

The wand of light has a Hardness of 5 and 2 hit points. It relies on rechargeable batteries with a 10-hour capacity. (Snarf's batteries ran out, but Aveeare was able to recharge them using his own power cells.) It can be used as a bludgeoning weapon with a –4 non-proficiency penalty, and inflicts 1d4 points of damage on a successful hit.

WAND OF WISHING (Minor Magical Artifact)

Etheah's not telling, but in return for her good deeds, some powerful being granted her a magical wand that works only in her hands. She used it in the name of good, making her own wishes for the cause and granting wishes to those who would help her. Eventually this became an annoyance to Suthaze, who stole the wand to put an end to her "goody-two-shoes" ways. Etheah charged Snarf and Prince Raffendorf with the task of retrieving her wand, and they did so at great peril. It is now in Etheah's hands once more.

The wand functions very much like a *ring of three wishes* with a few important differences. The wand works for Etheah alone. All she must do is silently think a simple phrase and then point the wand at the creature making the wish. The wand recharges itself at a rate of one wish every four months, to a maximum of three wishes.

WIND-SPLITTING SWORD (Magical Sword)

Originally a trusty weapon of the noble Lord Windyarm, Telerie took the sword when her father was mortally wounded by the evil wizard Gathgor. She used it throughout her career, finally wielding it to battle Gathgor at Snarf's side. Telerie continues to carry her family legacy on future adventures.

The wind-splitting sword acts as a +2 longsword with a special spell-deflection ability. Any spell that targets the wielder or his square requiring line of effect (see Core Rulebook I, Chapter 10, Casting a Spell) can be deflected with a Reflex saving throw (DC equal to 10 plus the caster's level). A deflected spell will travel its full range (as if the wielder had cast the spell) in a random direction. To determine the direction, roll on the Grenadelike Weapon table (see Player's Handbook, Chapter 8, Grenadelike Weapon Attacks). If the saving throw is failed, it takes effect normally.

Caster Level: 13th; *Prerequisites:* Craft Magic Arms & Armor, Spell turning. *Market Price:* 190,315 gp.

Chapter 5:
Monsters, Critters, and Creatures

The SnarfQuest lands are home to mundane animals, exotic creatures, and every variation in-between. Snarf and his companions encountered many creatures common to fantasy literature and gaming, but many were unique to the world.

D20 SYSTEM CREATURES IN SNARFQUEST

Just about any creature from Core Rulebook III can be included in a SnarfQuest campaign, usually with a small twist or hook to make them appropriate to the style and tone of the world. Here are some of the monsters that Snarf met during the "Quest for the Throne" storyline:

— Snarf was a terrible host to the first orc he met, who he frightened and then robbed at the beginning of his quest.

— While certainly not an ordinary red dragon, Willie was the guard of Suthaze's treasury. When Snarf broke the identity crisis spell, the dragon's original personality of Kizarvexius was briefly restored. Forever brain-damaged by the destruction of Suthaze's tower, Willie is now convinced he is a duck.

— Suthaze followed the tradition of many evil fantasy wizards before him and had a cadre of orcs as henchmen and guards. Unfortunately, the majority of them were in Suthaze's tower during Willie/Kizarvexius's rampage. Any survivors were surely killed when the tower exploded.

— Snarf thought he saw a silver dragon falling from the sky. It turned out to be Aveeare's spaceship making a crash landing.

— Telerie easily outmatched the gnoll sentry at the gates of Gathgor's keep, defeating it under three rounds of combat!

— Gathgor's keep held even more surprises for Snarf, Aveeare, and Telerie—including a yowling wraith waiting behind a door.

— In the "lost" episode set sometime in the future, we see a baron who turns himself into a werewolf and goes on a bloody prowl until defeated by Snarf and Telerie.

I think the main reason I mixed some of the D&D creatures in Snarf's world is because when I was doing the Snarf strip, I was involved in a big D&D game with my fellow artists at TSR. I could have used more D&D creatures but I didn't want to get involved in a copyright dispute with TSR. I didn't know what monsters were public domain, or which ones TSR owned all the rights to, so I tried to keep most of the monsters generic. I always wanted to do a Beholder in the strip. I am sure I could have had some great laughs with that.

NEW CREATURES

In addition to the more familiar creatures seen in the monthly adventures of Snarf, there were a host of creatures new and strange. Foot-eating gophers, deadly leeches, and garbage-disposal lizards are all a part of the young lands.

CAVEBITER

Medium Beast

Hit Dice: 3d10+6 (22 hp)

Initiative: +0

Speed: 30 ft.

AC: 14 (+4 natural)

Attacks: Bite +6 melee

Damage: Bite 2d6+3

Face/Reach: 5 ft. / 5 ft.

Special Attacks: Head butt

Special Qualities: Scent

Saves: Fort +5, Ref +3, Will +1

Abilities: Str 16, Dex 10, Con 14, Int 2, Wis 10, Cha 14

Skills: Climb +4, Listen +5, Spot +5

Feats: Weapon focus (bite)

Climate/Terrain: Any subterranean

Organization: Solitary, pair, family (2-5), or pack (5-20)

Challenge Rating: 1

Treasure: None

Alignment: Always neutral

Advancement: 4 to 5 HD (Medium); 6 to 10 HD (Large)

Cavebiters are hideous underground reptiles with the intelligence and personalities of dogs. A cavebiter is a strange-looking creatures, obviously a reptile, but possessing a comical doglike appearance as well—including a panting tongue and dog-shaped nose. It walks on all fours but sits in an upright position. Its head is hideously large when compared to its body, making it move awkwardly but also granting the bite of a much larger creature. The 'biter has flared ears and bony spikes on the top of its well-armored head.

Cavebiters live in caves and underground tunnels, often living the whole of their lives without ever seeing the light of day. Some took advantage of the creature's dog-like personality and trained them to be guard animals.

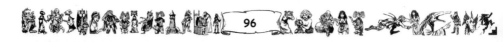

Combat

Cavebiters are territorial pack creatures, attempting to drive off intruders with teeth-baring growls. If that doesn't work, the creature will attack with full ferocity, first dazing its opponent with a head-butt, then biting with its massive jaws.

Head Butt (Ex): They say no one expects a head-butt, and when a cavebiter uses this attack it's certainly true. A cavebiter can make a head-butt attack with a charge action, using its bite melee attack bonus but inflicting 1d6+3 points of damage. Medium-size or smaller creatures must make a Fortitude saving throw (DC 12) or become dazed for 1d4 rounds.

Nolmer's Notes

Snarf had been badly injured by the mountain giant and was still convinced he was a heroic honey bee. When the group encountered a cavebiter in the dark (very possibly set by Gathgor as a guard), Snarf immediately "stung" it to death with his sword, winning the swordswoman Telerie's admiration.

CLAWGROWLER

Small Humanoid (Reptilian)

Hit Dice: 1d8+5 (7 hp)

Initiative: +2 (Dex)

Speed: 30 ft.

AC: 15 (+1 size, +2 Dex, +2 natural)

Attacks: Short sword +3 melee

Damage: Short sword 1d6-1

Face/Reach: 5 ft./5 ft.

Saves: Fort +2, Ref +4, Will -1

Abilities: Str 8, Dex 14, Con 14, Int 6, Wis 8, Cha 12

Skills: Hide +8, Listen +1, Move Silently +4, Spot +1

Feats: Weapon finesse (short sword)

Climate/Terrain: Any warm land

Organization: Solitary, gang (4-9), band (10-100 plus 100% noncombatants plus 1 2nd level warrior per twenty adults and 1 leader of 3rd-5th level)

Challenge Rating: 1/2

Treasure: Standard

Alignment: Usually lawful evil

Advancement: By character class

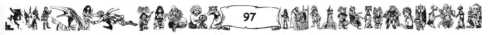

Clawgrowlers are small evil humanoids. Originating from the Beast Mountains and menacing civilized folk wherever they go, Clawgrowlers relish combat even when the odds are hopelessly against them.

Vicious little reptiles who live for their next battle, they are universally hated by elves, dwarves, and men. They are almost always found in the Beast Mountains, though some individuals have left their bands and met up with other, unscrupulous folk who will use them.

Clawgrowlers speak a crude form of Common.

Combat

Clawgrowlers love combat, and commonly wield short swords or daggers. They enjoy cutting their enemies to ribbons and watching the blood flow.

Clawgrowlers possess low-light vision.

Nolmer's Notes

Snarf and Aveeare were on the road to the city of Keynovia when they were accosted by bandits. The bandit leader's henchmen was a clawgrowler named "Twitch," who Aveeare wasted no time in dispatching.

DARK SHADE DEATH LEECH

Diminutive Beast

Hit Dice: 1d10+3 (4 hp)

Initiative: +6 (Dex, Improved Initiative)

Speed: 10 ft.

AC: 16 (+4 size, +2 Dex)

Attacks: Bite +6 melee

Damage: Bite 1d2-1

Face/Reach: 1 ft. / 0 ft.

Special Attacks: Blood drain, poison

Saves: Fort +2, Ref +4, Will +1

Abilities: Str 8, Dex 14, Con 11, Int 12, Wis 12, Cha 14

Skills: Climb +3, Hide +6, Listen +5, Move Silently +6, Spot +5, Swim +3

Feats: Improved Initiative, Toughness, Weapon finesse (bite)

*Climate/Terra*in: Any temperate or tropical

Organization: Solitary

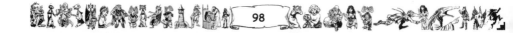

Challenge Rating: —

Treasure: None

Alignment: Usually neutral

Advancement: _ HD (Diminutive); 1 to 2 HD (Tiny)

Silent, stealthy killers in the wild, the intelligent and trainable dark shade death leeches are valued by assassins for their deadly poison bite.

A dark shade death leech looks like a diminutive, purple, land-bound octopus with large eyes. While it has numerous tentacles, it also has one with a crab-like claw it uses to grip. Its mouth is usually hidden on its underbelly, with large fangs. Like most leeches, the dark shade variety subsists on blood. Though they are adequate swimmers and spawn in water, dark shade death leeches can live almost anywhere (provided the temperature is not too cold).

Very few are aware of this, but dark shade death leeches are both smarter and stronger than any creature so small has any right to be. If around humanoids, they will pick up languages quickly, although they possess no vocal cords to allow any response other than physical gestures.

Combat

Dark shade death leeches often hunt by climbing to a high perch and then dropping down on their preys. They kill their victims with a fatally poison bite, then drink while the blood is still fresh.

Blood Drain (Ex): A dark shade death leech can attack itself for blood drain as a full attack action. For each round it remains attached, it deals 1d2 points of temporary Constitution damage. A leech can drink up to 4 points of Constitution before becoming gorged. A poisoned creature can still provide adequate blood, even after death.

Poison (Ex): The death leech's poison delivers a powerful toxin, requiring a Fortitude save (DC 11, Initial 2d6 Con/Secondary 2d6 Con).

I like to take very minor characters and let them have a greater impact in the course of the adventure. Subplots are very important. The Death Leech was one of them. He is a highly intelligent creature but no one knew it. I don't think Gabul had a clue. I imagine the ol' leech was feeding every time he was placed on the gagglezoomers back. The leech is basically a blood sucker but can survive on other foods. He doesn't have to kill when he feeds. He can release venom through his fangs only when necessary. Basically I see the dark shade death leeches as being kind of laid back. They will put up with a lot of crap without taking drastic actions, and will never bite to kill unless it is the last resort.

Nolmer's Notes

Gabul the transportation merchant sold a dark shade death leech to Snarf in the city of Keynovia, calling it a "gaggaleech." (It is unknown whether the slick merchant knew of the leech's true nature.) The leech showed both remarkable intelligence and willpower, becoming an important figure in Snarf's future adventures.

GAGGLEZOOMER

Large Beast

Hit Dice: 6d8+30 (57 hp)

Initiative: -1 (Dex)

Speed: 120 ft.

AC: 14 (-1 size, -1 Dex, +6 natural)

Attacks: Bite +8 melee

Damage: Bite 1d8+5

Face/Reach: 5 ft. by 10 ft./5 ft.

Special Qualities: Running endurance, spinal sensitivity

Saves: Fort +10, Ref +4, Will +2

Abilities: Str 20, Dex 8, Con 20, Int 2, Wis 10, Cha 6

Skills: Listen +2, Spot +2

Feats: Run

Climate/Terrain: Any non-arctic

Organization: Solitary

Challenge Rating: 3

Treasure: None

Alignment: Always neutral

Advancement: 7 to 8 HD (Large); 8 to 12 HD (Huge)

"Now let me tell ya 'bout a gagglezoomer. They are the fastest an' dumbest animal alive... they will never move from one spot unless somethin' just barely touches his back, that is the most sensitive part of his body. The rest of his body is hard as a rock. He can exist for days without food or water.

"In the wild, a gagglezoomer will sit in one spot until a leaf or insect lands on his back. Then he will immediately run at a breakneck speed in a random direction until whatever was on his back gets off, then he will immediately stop... dead still! Gagglezoomers are very rare... but they have a long life span unless they run off a mountain or somethin' like that."

—Gabull, Merchant of Transportation

Gagglezoomers are placid, peaceful creatures that spend their days quietly grazing, barely moving—until something touches their highly sensitive backs and they burst into incredible speed, capable of going non-stop for weeks.

While some use gagglezoomers for transportation, it is quite rare as controlling these creatures is extremely difficult. They run very fast and for long periods of time, but they do not slow down before stopping—usually causing damage to both people and property. That said, gagglezoomers are capable of taking travelers down the road faster than any other beast known in the young lands.

In the wild, 'zoomers (as they are sometimes called) live in herds, quietly grazing until one runs off because an insect has landed on its back. Rainwater doesn't seem to cause any discomfort to a gagglezoomer's back, but other types of weather does. "As dangerous as a herd of gagglezoomers in a hailstorm" is a common saying in Keynovia and Quessa.

Combat

Gagglezoomers generally do not fight, though it may bite something that hurts it or pesters it. The damage a 'zoomer usually does is caused by impact into buildings and other solid objects (since it will not stop—even when it's about to run into a wall—unless the object on its back is removed). A gagglezoomer hitched to a cart or wagon also usually causes damage when it stops, unless the driver is smart enough to stop it in an area where the 'zoomer will slide to a halt (such as sand or mud). A 'zoomer's feet have enough traction to come to a dead stop in most types of terrain.

Running Endurance (Ex): Gagglezoomers are capable of running at full speed continuously for one day per point of Constitution ability. Once this time has elapsed, the beast will collapse—exhausted. A worn out gagglezoomer requires twenty-four hours of rest before running again.

I loved the Gagglezoomer; I created it because I had to solve a problem. I had to create a way for the heroes to travel faster so that they could go to far off places and experience different geography as well. Teleportation was an easy way, but I didn't want to give a character that much power. If they could travel at least 60 miles per hour, then that would solve the problem. I wracked my lil' ol' brain. Being from the South, we have a lot of old sayings that embellish our speech. For example; "don't look a gift horse in the mouth," or, "he looks like he has been beaten with an ugly stick." I have often wondered who or how these old sayings got started and thought that there was probably a funny story behind each of them. As I wracked my brain, a new "old saying" came to my mind. I imagined someone looking really roughed up, like he had a bad night and saying "man, we had a wild party last night" and someone asks, "how wild was it?" The reply would be, " as wild as a herd of gagglezoomers in a hail storm". So I started creating a wacky animal that could run fast, in random directions and very hard to control. Thus the gagglezoomer was created.

Spinal Sensitivity (Ex): Most of the gagglezoomer's body is tough, but the discolored area on its back is highly sensitive. Anything heavier than a snowflake touching the area will cause the gagglezoomer to begin running at full speed (five times its normal movement rate). The beast will not stop until the offending object has been removed or until itself collapses from exhaustion.

Nolmer's Notes

If Snarf had not been drinking during his visit to Keynovia, perhaps he would not have chosen such a dangerous animal. Still, Snarf is not easily discouraged, and even after being injured by the beast several times, he refused to give up—eventually becoming quite proficient in driving it. Certainly Snarf would have not been able to cross the Plains of Wafoo so quickly without it. Perhaps Snarf would still have his '"zoomer" to this day, had it not fallen into the Perpetual Pit.

GIANT, MOUNTAIN
Huge Giant

Hit Dice: 16d8+96 (168 hp)

Initiative: -2 (Dex)

Speed: 50 ft.

AC: 16 (-2 size, -2 Dex, +10 natural)

Attacks: Huge greatclub +19/+14 melee

Damage: Huge greatclub 2d6+10

Face/Reach: 10 ft. by 10 ft./15 ft.

Special Attacks: Great swing

Saves: Fort +16, Ref +3, Will +5

Abilities: Str 30, Dex 6, Con 22, Int 6, Wis 10, Cha 11

Skills: Climb +20, Jump +13, Spot +3, Swim +13

Feats: Cleave, Power Attack, Weapon Focus (greatclub)

Climate/Terrain: Any hill, mountainous

Organization: Solitary

Challenge Rating: 10

Treasure: Standard

Alignment: Often chaotic evil

Advancement: By character class

Mountain giants inhabit the foothills and peaks of the jagged mountain ranges of the young lands, using their size and strength to bully others outside their home territory. Mountain giants are huge creatures, standing twenty feet tall with thick muscles and large

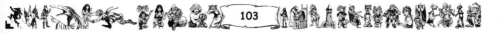

guts. They wear little or no clothing to cover their hairy bodies. Their hairless faces are marked by unkempt hair, flat noses, and an underbite that emphasizes their lower fangs. These creatures are infrequently encountered, but they still pose a hazard to caravans, mountain-folk, and adventurers. Fiercely territorial, a mountain giant does not tolerate any trespassers, including (and especially) other mountain giants. It usually gives others a chance to flee, but will not hesitate to kill and eat anyone who is foolish enough to stay once they've been given a warning.

Combat

All strength and no finesse, a mountain giant lumbers into combat with its crude (but tremendous) homemade club. It eats humanoid or animal kills, but usually will not give chase if its opponents flee.

Great Swing (Ex): A mountain giant can use its greatclub and incredible strength to send its enemies flying. It can perform a greatswing as a full-attack action if it has its full reach against an opponent (15 ft.). Any creature of Medium-size or smaller will suffer normal damage and be flung backwards in an arc 2d6x10 feet plus 10 feet for each point of the giant's Strength modifier (+10). Upon landing (or crashing into a barrier) the creature suffers another 2d6 points of falling damage.

Mountain giants possess darkvision with a range of 60 feet.

Nolmer's Notes

After nearly perishing in the Perpetual Pit, Snarf encountered a mountain giant in the path to Gathgor's Keep. The giant won the first bout, in which Snarf was not only sent flying but also knocked silly. A delirious Snarf, thinking he was a gagglezoomer, ran back toward the giant before the leech suggested that he was a honey bee. Snarf "bee" stung the giant with his sword (several times in its hairy belly), then nimbly dodged to the side, letting the creature's own clumsiness defeat itself.

GRABGOBBLER

Tiny Beast
Hit Dice: 1d10+3 (5 hp)
Initiative: +3 (Dex)
Speed: 30 ft., burrow 10 ft.
AC: 15 (+2 size, +3 Dex)
Attacks: Bite +3 melee, 2 claws -2 melee
Damage: Bite 1d3-1, 2 claws 1d2-1
Face/Reach: 2 _ ft. / 0 ft.
Special Attacks: Improved grab
Special Qualities: Scent

Saves: Fort +3, Ref +4, Will +0

Abilities: Str 8, Dex 14, Con 13, Int 2, Wis 10, Cha 12

Skills: Hide +8, Listen +6

Feats: Toughness, Weapon finesse (bite, claws)

Climate/Terrain: Any forest or plains

Organization: Solitary, pair, or family (2-5)

Challenge Rating: 1/2

Treasure: None

Alignment: Always neutral

Advancement: –

Grabbgobblers are relentless badger-like creatures that dig burrows and then lie in wait, grabbing from above and pulling a prey down into the hole where it can be devoured.

These dirt-digging critters are sometimes called "angry gophers" for their habits and demeanor, or "yeebeegeebees" for the strange sounds they make when angry. They are best known for their foul disposition and painful bite.

Combat

Grabgobblers dig under soft patches of ground, then wait and listen for prey. While it usually attacks only creatures smaller than itself, a grabgobbler will sometimes grab the feet of larger creatures and attack out of hunger and spite.

Improved Grab (Ex): A grabgobbler can use this ability when it hits a creature with its bite attack. It will immediately drag a Tiny or smaller creature into its hole, or the foot of a Small or Medium creature. It can maintain its bite, inflicting automatic bite damage each round until it lets go.

Grabgobblers gain a +4 racial bonus to Hide and Listen checks. Grabgobblers possess low-light vision.

Nolmer's Notes

Snarf had barely begun his quest for the throne when he met Raffendorf, a human prince magically transformed into a half-man, half-rat. The Prince's foot was caught by a grabgobbler, and begged for Snarf's aid. Once Snarf freed Raffendorf from the dangerous creature, the two became companions and made their way for the Tower of Suthaze.

WHAZZAT LIZARD

Small Beast

Hit Dice: 1d10+3 (8 hp)

Initiative: +2 (Dex)

Speed: 20 ft.

AC: 15 (+1 size, +2 Dex, +2 natural)

Attacks: Bite -1 melee

Damage: Bite 1d4-2

Face/Reach: 5 ft. / 5 ft.

Special Qualities: Digest anything, scent

Saves: Fort +5, Ref +4, Will +0

Abilities: Str 6, Dex 14, Con 16, Int 3,
Wis 11, Cha 10

Skills: Listen +4, Spot +2

Climate/Terrain: Any warm land

Organization: Solitary, pair, or family (2-5)

Challenge Rating: 1/3

Treasure: None

Alignment: Always neutral

Advancement: -

Whazzat lizards are scavengers and scroungers, able to digest items other creatures find impossible. Their name is derived from the sound they make, which amazingly resembles "What's that?" spoken in Common.

The small, strange lizards of the old young lands are colorful, with specimens known to be blue, green, or even pink. They stand two-and-a-half feet tall, with long two-toed feet but possessing remarkably humanoid-like hands (including opposable thumbs). Whazzat lizards have long necks counterbalanced by their tails, and walk slightly hunched forward.

The idea of a whazzat lizard came from my son Jeremy. At the time I was doing the SQ strip he was around 3 years old and at the age of asking questions. No matter what was said to him, he would ask "why" or "what's that". Sometimes he could drive ya crazy! I could be doing something or on the phone and he would ask, "What's that?" over and over again, nonstop!!!

Some birds make sounds like "bob white" or "whip-poor-will," so the idea came to me; what if there was this little lizard thing and he made only one sound that sounded like "whazzat?" Wouldn't that just drive you crazy? And it nearly drove Snarf crazy.

A whazzat lizard has a digestive system and appetite to rival goats. They can eat and derive nutrients from nearly anything, although they will spend time scrounging for items that taste good to them. Apparently, the higher gold piece value of an item, the better its taste to a whazzat lizard. A lizard will eat anything vegetable or inorganic, but will not eat an animal—living or dead.

Though considered stupid beasts by most people in the young lands, whazzat lizards are slightly smarter than other animals. If properly trained, they could become useful and loyal companions.

Combat

Whazzat lizards are peaceful non-meat eaters. They will run if attacked, and bite only if cornered.

Digest Anything (Ex): A whazzat lizard has an amazing digestive system. It can digest anything it chooses to eat (including diamonds, gold coins, or anything else small enough for it to swallow whole). This gives a whazzat lizard a +8 racial bonus to Fortitude saving throws against poison and other ingested substances. As Snarf found out, anything by a whazzat does not eventually pass through.

Whazzat lizards possess low-light vision.

Nolmer's Notes

King Snarf nearly met his end at the Perpetual Pit, and a pair of whazzat lizards wandered over to see the commotion stemmed from Snarf and his companion hanging at the edge of the pit! When the lizards made things more difficult, Snarf considered slaying them immediately, but opted for mercy. Later, the lizard became both mount and friend to the leech in Snarf's adventures.

YOWLER

Tiny Beast

Hit Dice: 1/4th d10 (1 hp)

Initiative: +1 (Dex)

Speed: 20 ft.

AC: 15 (+2 size, +2 Dex, +2 natural)

Attacks: Bite -2 melee

Damage: Bite 1d3-4

Face/Reach: 2 _ ft./0 ft.

Special Attacks: Yowl

Saves: Fort +3, Ref +3, Will -1

Abilities: Str 2, Dex 12, Con 12, Int 2, Wis 8, Cha 14

Skills: Listen +3, Spot +3
Climate/Terrain: Any warm land
Organization: Solitary or pair
Challenge Rating: 1/6
Treasure: None
Alignment: Always neutral
Advancement: -

Yowlers are tiny, harmless lizards that are only noteworthy for the loud and horrifying screech they make when frightened.

A green lizard standing barely over a foot tall, a yowler spends its day digging for worms and grubs. It is physically unable to defend itself against predators, so it relies completely on its overdeveloped vocal cords.

Combat

Yowlers only eat fine vermin. It may bite if handled, but is not capable of inflicting much damage. If a yowler feels threatened (or is just bored), it will screech ("yowl").

Yowl (Ex): A yowler can produce a horrifying sound—long and loud, it varies from a deep rumble to a high-pitched shriek. It can yowl as a full-round action that provokes an attack of opportunity, but creatures less than 5 Hit Die must make a Will save (DC 12) or become shaken for 2d4 rounds. (Negate the effect if a creature realizes the source for the sound.)

Yowlers possess low-light vision.

Nolmer's Notes

After bravely defeating the dark rider, Snarf and Raffendorf traveled on a moonless night. They heard a terrible wail which sent them running, convinced a horrible monster was after them. Scared witless by a yowl virtually right before them, they quickly realized it was a yowler and splattered the critter.

Chapter 6:
Cast of Characters

Snarf started his quest alone, but quickly made friends and enemies—a list including several beautiful women, two evil wizards, a prince, a princess, two robots, and a confused dragon, just to name a few! In addition to the stats and descriptions of the heroes and villains of SnarfQuest, this chapter provides examples of the people one might meet in an ongoing campaign set in Snarf's world.

AVEEARE (VR-X9-4-M2 Galactic Probe)

Robot

CR 4; Medium-size Construct; HD 8d10; hp 60; Init +6 (Dex, Improved Initiative); Spd 20 ft.; AC 20 (+1 size, +3 Dex, +6 dermal plating); Ranged +9/+9 Laser (2d10/crit x2/Rng 100 ft.) or +9/+9 Electroblaster (2d10 subdual/crit x2/Rng 50 ft.); AL: LG; SQ Robot; SV Fort -, Ref +6, Will +4; Str 16, Dex 16, Con -, Int 20, Wis 14, Cha 14.

    Skills and Feats: Astrogation (Space) +11, Climb +9, Diplomacy +8, Knowledge (Starship Operations) +11, Knowledge (Galactic History) +11, Listen +9, Navigation (Time) +11, Pilot +9, Search +11, Spot +9; Ambidexterity, Combat Reflexes, Improved Initiative, Point Blank Shot, Rapid Shot.

    Possessions: Electroblasters (2), Lasers (2), Visual Sensors (Standard, Low-Light, Infrared)

    Notes: Aveeare is immune to mind-influencing effects (charms, compulsions, phantasms, patterns, and morale effects) and to poison, sleep, paralysis, stunning, disease, death and necromantic effects. Robots are not subject to critical hits, subdual damage, ability damage, ability drain, or energy drain. They are immune to anything requiring a Fortitude save (unless the effect also works on objects). Robots do not "die," but when reduced to 0 hit points or less, they are immediately destroyed. Since it was never alive, a robot cannot be raised or resurrected. Aveeare has low-light vision and darkvision with a range of 60 feet.

    History: A VR-X94M2 Galactic Probe (Government Issue Robot) was originally part of an unmanned historical survey mission from the far future. When its ship malfunctioned, the robot was stranded in the old young lands and encountered Snarf. The zeetvah could not understand the VR-X9 designation, so took to calling the robot "Aveeare." Snarf convinced Aveeare that he was a person destined for importance, so the robot decided to follow Snarf to record how he would shape the future of the world. While Snarf believed Aveeare is a half-crazy, armored wizard, he also has come to trust and value the robot as both ally and friend. Aveeare accompanied Snarf through Keynovia, helped liberate the city of Quessa, risked the dangers of the Perpetual Pit, assisted in the defeat of the wizard Gathgor, and was crucial to Snarf's ascension to the throne. Aveeare has now acquired a new ship capable of both space- and time-travel, as well as a robot companion—a maintenance 'bot nicknamed "Effim."

Personality: Unlike early model robots, Aveeare has a distinct personality and is capable of understanding humor. Aveeare is programmed to record history, though damage from the crash and exposure to a primitive culture has veered it from that path (just a bit). It is loyal and helpful, ready to follow Snarf's lead even though it understands it is far more intelligent than the zeetvah. It only uses its weapons in self-defense or in defense of others. Aveeare is intensely curious about this primitive world, and has discovered things unknown to history (such as magic).

THE DARK RIDER

Adult Male Human
Ftr 5: CR 5; Medium-size Humanoid (human); HD 5d10+15; hp 45; Init +2 (Dex); Spd 20 ft.; AC 17 (+7 half-plate); Melee +9 Battleaxe (1d8+5/crit x3); AL: NE; SV Fort +7, Ref +3, Will +2; Str 16, Dex 14, Con 16, Int 10, Wis 12, Cha 9.

Skills and Feats: Handle Animal +7, Intimidate +2, Ride +12, Spot +2; Improved Mounted Combat, Martial Weapon Proficiency, Mounted Combat, Power Attack, Ride-By Attack, Weapon Focus (Battleaxe), Weapon Specialization (Battleaxe).

Possessions: Half-Plate, Battleaxe, Dagger, Warhorse (Light), Barding (Half-Plate).
History: Once a knight in the service of the king of Quessa, the now-exiled dark rider (whose name is known by a rare few) has used his martial skills to kill, rob, and terrorize others. It was just another ordinary day in the Beast Mountain lowlands when he spotted a lone zeetvah—an easy target. Luck was on the zeetvah's side, and the dark rider was defeated. Unable to accept the humiliation, the rider has been tracking Snarf for almost a year, hearing more about his exploits. Eventually he might get his revenge. Until then, there are many ways to earn gold.

Personality: Arrogant and rude, the dark rider is not polite dinner company. He is a highly effective warrior, however—especially on his white charger. His goals are simple: acquire wealth and power. But he cannot let his defeat at the hands of Snarf rest. He will seek the zeetvah out and finish what he started.

DORQUE DA WANDERER

Adult Male Human (Ugly)

Com 1, War 1: CR 1; Medium-size Humanoid (human); HD 1d4+1d8+2; hp 9; Init -1 (Dex); Spd 30 ft.; AC 9 (-1 Dex); Melee +1 Shortspear (1d8/crit x3) or Thrown +0 Shortspear (1d8/crit x3); AL: N; SV Fort +5, Ref -1, Will -1; Str 11, Dex 9, Con 13, Int 7, Wis 8, Cha 11.

Skills and Feats: Climb +1, Listen +0, Spot +0, Swim -1; Great Fortitude, Run.

Possessions: Shield (Small Wooden/Carried on back), Dagger, Shortspear.

History: Dorque's past is shrouded in mystery... though that is mostly because Dorque has such a lousy memory. After being fired from every job in his village, he figured that he must be destined to become a mercenary (since he was such a failure at everything else). With only his spear, dagger, and wits (or lack thereof), he set off into the wilderness... and promptly became lost. He spent the better part of a year stumbling around in the forest, until finally running into Snarf and Aveeare. At first the zeetvah wanted nothing to do with Dorque, who began following the pair. ("I follow you 'cause you is goin' someplace.") Snarf finally relented and offered Dorque a job for one silver piece a week. Snarf took a liking to Dorque as he and Snarf went on a drinking/shopping spree in Keynovia. When the group first tried to master the art of driving a gagglezoomer, they attracted the attention of the Keynovian guards. Dorque decided to "give dose guards a lil' lip," and like every other decision he has ever made, it ended badly. Dorque fell from Snarf's wagon and was arrested by the guards. Currently Dorque is the model prisoner, waiting patiently for the boss (Snarf) to rescue him.

Personality: Dorque isn't attractive, strong, intelligent, or talented. He has spent his life unloved and disliked, making decisions that have ended in disaster. The two traits that actually serve him well are loyalty and stubbornness. Snarf has treated Dorque better than anyone else had in the world, and Dorque firmly believes he will be reunited with the "boss" one day.

> Some people have asked me who or what Dorque is and why he is in the story. Old Dorque is just an ugly little stupid man. One reason he appears in the strip is to show that, although Snarf may be a bit hot headed, talk big, and thinks he is tough, he does have a heart. I guess Snarf eventually just felt sorry for old Dorque. The other reason is that through my life I have ran into a couple of people that became my friend whether I liked it or not and they drove me crazy. It seemed like nothing went right in their life and their problems always became mine. I felt sorry for them and didn't have the heart to dump them, but somehow they would disappear from my life just as quickly as they came.

EFFIM (FM94763-3X817 Maintenance Robot)

Robot

CR 2; Small-size Construct; HD 4d10; hp 30; Init +0; Spd 20 ft.; AC 15 (+1 size, +0 Dex, +4 dermal plating); Melee +5 Slam (1d4+2); AL: LN; SQ Robot, Improved Grab; SV Fort -, Ref +1, Will +1; Str 14, Dex 10, Con -, Int 14, Wis 10, Cha 10.

Skills and Feats: Astrogation (Space) +6, Climb +4, Diplomacy +4, Knowledge (Starship Operations) +8, Knowledge (Engineering) +8, Navigation (Time) +6, Pilot +2, Repair Tech +8, Search +4, Spot +2; Ambidexterity.

Notes: Effim is immune to mind-influencing effects (charms, compulsions, phantasms, patterns, and morale effects) and to poison, sleep, paralysis, stunning, disease, death effects, and necromantic effects. Robots are not subject to critical hits, subdual damage, ability damage, ability drain, or energy drain. They are immune to anything that requires a Fortitude save (unless the effect also works on objects). Robots are not at risk from death by massive damage, but when reduced to 0 hit points or less, they are immediately destroyed. Since it was never alive, a robot cannot be raised or resurrected. Effim has low-light vision and darkvision with a range of 60 feet.

History: "Effim" (as Snarf calls him) is a maintenance robot assigned to a ship, and was relatively unsophisticated until Fred—the ship's newest pilot and operator—added some sophisticated programs to give the robot personality and potentially useful skills. After Fred disappeared, Effim met and began taking orders from Aveerare—who as a Galactic Probe 'bot has rank and authority over a simple maintenance drone. Because Aveeare follows Snarf's lead, Effim has begun to do the same. The maintenance robot has as hard a time understanding a medieval world of magic as Snarf does comprehending the futuristic world of the robots.

Personality: Effim is designed to be enthusiastic and helpful. Unfortunately, while he is intelligent, Effim is not as quick to learn and adapt to new situations as Aveeare. Effim trusts everyone and will not become suspicious of anyone without obvious evidence that they mean harm.

ETHEAH OF THE WOODLAND

Adult Female Human

Sor 8: CR 8; Medium-size Humanoid (human); HD 8d4; hp 22; Init +1 (Dex); Spd 30 ft.; AC 11 (+1 Dex); AL: NG; SA Spells; SV Fort +2, Ref +3, Will +7; Str 9, Dex 12, Con 10, Int 15, Wis 13, Cha 15.

Skills and Feats: Concentration +8, Knowledge (Arcana) +12, Listen +6, Search +7, Spellcraft +10, Spot +6; Brew Potion, Craft Wondrous Item, Quicken Spell, Silent Spell.

Possessions: Clothes, Jewelry, Etheah's Wand of Wishing (see New Magical Items, Chapter Two).

Spells Known: Sorcerer (6 /7 /7 /5 /3)

0-Dancing Lights, Daze, Detect Magic, Light, Mage Hand, Mending, Open/Close, Read Magic

1-Color Spray, Identify, Protection from Evil, Sleep, Unseen Servant

2-Daylight, Invisibility, Locate Object

3-Clairaudience/Clairvoyance, Dispel Magic

4-Dimension Door.

History: Etheah left her native land behind long ago to pursue the magical arts in solitude. She has become a local champion of good in the region, using her magic to benefit others. As a reward for her good deeds she acquired a special wand of wishing (see New Magical Items, Chapter Two) that works only for her. Angered by her interference in his evil plans, the wizard Suthaze raided her home and stole her wand of wishing. She was still weeping over its loss when a zeetvah and human-sized rat (Snarf and Raffendorf, respectively) volunteered to help. Though she did not foresee much chance of success, she offered them each a wish if they returned her wand to her. Amazingly, the pair did return with the wand, plus a young almeer named Geezel, whom she gave a wish as well. The rat and zeetvah wasted their wishes, but Geezel had one with definite consequences: "I wish dat Etheah would fall in love wif me so much dat she wants me to stay here wif her to study magic so dat I may become a good, powerful wizard." From then on, Etheah fell in love with Geezel and feels a daily compulsion to study magic with him. She remains charitable, but also now longs for the day Geezel is old enough for the two of them to be wed.

Personality: Etheah is a good sorceress who desires to live in peace, but her strong sense of justice makes her dangerous when angered. Still, she prefers the subtle magics instead of flashy evocations. She is also generous with magical items to worthy champions, believing she's serving a good cause.

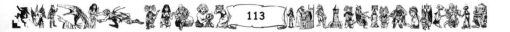

FRED, GALACTIC EXPLORER

Adult Male Alpha-Centauran

Exp 4; CR 2; Medium-size Humanoid (elf); HD 4d6+4; hp 18; Init +1 (Dex); Spd 30 ft.; AC 11 (+1 Dex); Melee +3 unarmed (1d2 subdual); AL: LG; SV Fort +2, Ref +2, Will +4; Str 11, Dex 12, Con 12, Int 14, Wis 10, Cha 12.

Skills and Feats: Astrogation (Space) +8, Diplomacy +5, Knowledge (Starship Operations) +9, Knowledge (Galactic History) +5, Intuit Direction +5, Listen +3, Navigation (Time) +9, Pilot +11, Search +5, Spot +3; Dodge ,Skill Focus (Pilot).

Possessions: Credit Cards, Futuristic Clothes, Wallet

History: When the unmanned expedition into the past did not return as scheduled, Fred was dispatched by the government to investigate. When he reached the past, Fred picked up the homing signal from the VR-X9-4-M2 and found the 'bot in the company of some of the primitive natives. He shut down the 'bot in order to remove the homing signal, but was then attacked by the natives! Bound and gagged, he was tied to the back of a strange lizard called a "gagglezoomer." Fred was determined to free himself and get his ship back—until the gagglezoomer started running and everything went black. Fred awoke, weeks later, with amnesia. He knows he isn't from "around here," and has vague nightmares of a dark-haired woman and a demonic creature with bat-wing ears, but cannot remember his own name or background. Fred is searching for clues to his past, and wondering why it does not feel right when people call him an "elf."

Personality: Fred's idea of exploring is doing everything from the cockpit of a space cruiser. New to the young lands, he was naive enough to let his guard down. Now he does-n't remember who he is, but his amiable personality has remained intact. He is a hard-worker and loyal friend, and he knows these traits served him well wherever he was orig-inally from!

GATHGOR

Old Male Human

Evo 9: CR 9; Medium-size Humanoid (human); HD 9d4; hp 30; Init +2 (Dex); Spd 30 ft.; AC 12 (+2 Dex); SA Spells; AL: LE; SV Fort +4, Ref +5, Will +6; Str 10, Dex 14, Con 10, Int 17, Wis 11, Cha 9.

Skills and Feats: Alchemy +8, Concentration +8, Gather Information +2, Intimidate +2, Knowledge (Arcana) +13, Knowledge (History) +7, Knowledge (Nobility and Royalty) +7, Listen +2, Search +5, Spellcraft +15, Spot +5; Combat Casting, Empower Spell, Enlarge Spell, Extend Spell, Quicken Spell, Scribe Scroll, Spell Focus (Evocation).

Spells Known: Wizard (4+1 /5+1 /5+1 /4+1 /2+1 /1+1)

- **0-** Arcane Mark, Dancing Lights, Detect Magic, Flare, Ghost Sound, Light, Mage Hand, Mending, Open/Close, Prestidigitation, Ray of Frost, Read Magic, Resistance
- **1-** Burning Hands, Color Spray, Mage Armor, Magic Missile, Reduce, Shield, Shocking Grasp, Summon Monster I
- **2-** Blindness/Deafness, Bull's Strength, Levitate, Melf's Acid Arrow, Protection from Arrows, Shatter, Web
- **3-** Dispel Magic, Fireball, Fly, Lightning Bolt, Sleet Storm, Wind Wall
- **4-** Fire Trap, Ice Storm, Minor Globe of Invulnerability, Shout, Wall of Fire
- **5-** Cloudkill, Cone of Cold, Fabricate

History: Gathgor has been greedy and power-hungry his entire life. Feigning scholarly interest, he learned magic from every master he could, before stealing their spellbooks and items for his own cause. Once he had driven away every other magic-user in the region, he built his own keep and hired humanoid mercenaries to be guards, spies, and assassins. Gathgor spent most of his time in seclusion, but would make raids on local lords and land-owners. He made a great mistake, however, when he raided the castle of Lord Windyarm. The lord's daughter was a young and attractive girl. Gathgor spared her, and plundered the family's fortune even though he failed to get the Windyarm's famed magical sword. The girl grew into both a beautiful woman and a powerful fighter, bent on revenge. When she brought the zeetvah Snarf, a "robot," a lizard, and a leech into the keep, Gathgor was unprepared. His last words were: "Where did all of these idiots come from?" Moments later, the fangs of a dark shade death leech entered his neck, and Gathgor was no more.

Personality: Gathgor was a grumpy, bossy, evil old man before his death—but also sharp and perceptive. He has a weak spot, too, for beautiful women, which is why he so easily recognized Telerie Windyarm after many years.

GEEZEL

Young Male Almeer (Nice)

Sor 1: CR 1; Small-size Humanoid (almeer, nice); HD 1d4; hp 4; Init +1 (Dex); Spd 20 ft.; AC 12 (+1 size, +1 Dex); AL: NG; SA Spells; SQ Fleet-footed; SV Fort +2, Ref +3, Will +7; Str 8, Dex 12, Con 10, Int 12, Wis 14, Cha 12.

Skills and Feats: Concentration +3, Hide +5, Knowledge (Arcana) +4, Listen +5, Scry +2, Spellcraft +4; Dodge.

Possessions: Clothes.

Spells Known: Sorcerer (5 / 4)

    0-Daze, Detect Magic, Light, Ray of Frost

    1-Jump, Shocking Grasp.

History: Like many of his kind, Geezel left his small clan to study magic in the greater world. Little more than a child, he followed rumors of a powerful wizard named Suthaze. Not knowing the time-jumping wizard's true nature, Geezel became Suthaze's apprentice. Most of Geezel's duties included feeding the guard-dragon (who liked fish) and watching the tower while the wizard time-jumped into the future. When Geezel accidentally broke Suthaze's magical time-jumping glass, he ran for it. Salvation came in the form of intruders—Snarf and Raffendorf. Geezel helped them find and return Etheah of the Woodland's wand of wishing. When the beautiful sorceress granted Geezel a wish, he quickly wished for Etheah to fall in love with him. Ever since that day, he has lived under Etheah's protection and has slowly been learning more of the ways of sorcery. One day, he knows, the two will be married.

Personality: Geezel is still very much a child, though he is smarter and wiser than most people give him credit for. Nothing makes Geezel angrier than when others underestimate him. Showing such people up is what Geezel loves best. The almeer is also very curious about the world, and would like to do more adventuring someday.

PENELOPE, FIRST KNIGHT OF THE ROBOT (Princess Penelope of Quessa)

Adult Female Human

Nob 3, Ftr 2, Robot 6: CR 11; Medium-size Humanoid (human); HD 3d8+2d10+6d8+22; hp 67; Init +0; Spd 20 ft.; AC 19 (+8 Full Plate); Melee +10/+5 Short Sword (1d6-1/crit 19-20); SA Deceptive Melee; SQ Improved Sleep Resistance, Great Endurance, Hunger Resistance; AL: LG; SV Fort +9, Ref +3, Will +8; Str 9, Dex 11, Con 15, Int 12, Wis 9, Cha 16.

    Skills and Feats: Balance -3, Climb +0, Hide -7, Jump -2, Knowledge (Fashion) +9, Knowledge (History) +11, Knowledge (Local) +3, Knowledge (Nobility & Royalty) +7, Listen +3, Move Silently -7, Ride +4, Search +5, Sense Motive +3, Spot +3; Combat Reflexes, Endurance, Great Fortitude, Iron Will, Mounted Combat, Skill Focus (Knowledge-History), Toughness, Weapon Finesse (Short Sword).

Possessions: "Robot" Full Plate Mail, Short Sword, portrait of St. Aveeare.

    History: Penelope is the oldest child born to the King and Queen of the city-state of Quessa. She spent the early part of her life pampered, sheltered, and spoiled. Every meal was multi-course, her bed made with down pillows and silken sheets. Her passions for creature com-

forts and fashion dominated her early life. Then the evil wizard Suthaze came to Quessa, with a terrifying red dragon under his control. The royal family was held hostage, and their lives seemed forfeit. Then he came: Aveeare. The strange little knight single-handedly defeated Suthaze and his dragon (well, there was a little help from a zeetvah—but not much). When offered rewards, including marriage to Penelope, Aveeare refused. "I am a robot," he intoned, explaining that he lived a life without food, drink, sleep, comfort, or marriage. Penelope realized then what a waste her spoiled life had been. When Aveeare left, she had already converted others to the robot's philosophy. Within a year, Aveeare was declared a saint by the newly formed Order of Robot, with Penelope leading the outfit. She began to knight worthy warriors, granting them armor and weapons, sending them on noble quests and admonishing them to not succumb to the needs of basic comfort. Their reward would be great. She hopes that St. Aveeare would be proud of her. She also wishes deep down that word of the Order of Robot will reach him, and that the strange little knight will one day return to her.

Personality: Once, Penelope was shallow and focused only on fashion and comfort. ("Like, we will set the fashion world on its ear. We'll be the trend setters.") But when Aveeare rebuffed her royal advances, she changed. Determined to follow in "St." Aveeare's footsteps, she now rejects basic comfort, food, water, and dedicates herself to the cause of good. She still yearns for Aveeare's return, and is eager for any news or rumors of his travels.

RAFFENDORF, EXILED HUMAN PRINCE

Adult Male Rat-Man (Altered)

Nob 2, Ftr 1: CR 3; Medium-size Humanoid (human); HD 2d8+1d10+6; hp 27; Init +1 (Dex); Spd 20 ft.; AC 17 (+1 Dex, +6 Banded Mail); Melee +4 Short Sword (1d6/crit 19-20); SA Deceptive Melee; AL: NG; SA Deceptive Melee; SQ Scent; SV Fort +4, Ref +1, Will +3; Str 11, Dex 12, Con 14, Int 12, Wis 11, Cha 13.

Skills and Feats: Bluff +7, Climb +3, Diplomacy +6, Gather Information +3, Innuendo +4, Jump +5, Knowledge (Geography) +4, Knowledge (History) +4, Knowledge (Local) +4, Knowledge (Nobility and Royalty) +4, Listen +6, Move Silently +4, Ride +3, Spot +4, Swim -5; Alertness, Run, Weapon Finesse (Short Sword), Weapon Focus (Short Sword).

Possessions: Banded Mail, Short Sword.

Notes: His half-rat form, Raffendorf receives a +2 racial bonus to Listen checks.

History: Originally a human prince from the city-state of Rada, Raffendorf ran away from home as a teenager to seek adventure—determined he

would be a hero-prince as sung by the bards. Instead he ran afoul of the evil wizard Suthaze, who punished him by turning him into a half-man, half-rat. His bad luck continued, with close calls that cost him his new tail and put out one of his eyes (now covered with an eyepatch). Just when things couldn't get much worse, a grabgobbler grabbed his foot while he was walking down a forest trail. That's when an ornery zeetvah named Snarf arrived on the scene, and saved Raffendorf's foot. The two became fast friends and companions, raiding Suthaze's tower and recovering Etheah's wand of wishing. Though tempted to join Snarf on more adventures, Raf was more resolved in becoming human again. He worked for Etheah an entire year to get another wish, but then learned that even Etheah's powerful wish magic was not strong enough to counter Suthaze's spell. Now he's spending some time in Zeetville, planning a new course.

Personality: Raffendorf likes to believe he is "tough and rugged," but he is still a child of nobility. He has learned to survive on his own in the wild, but prefers the company of others. Well-spoken and gallant, he does not tolerate bad manners. He likes Snarf, but feels the zeetvah is a bit crude for one aspiring to kingship. More than anything, he is sick of being a rat and direly wants to regain his human form.

SNARF (Snarfenja de'Gottago)

Adult Male Zeetvah

Ftr 4: CR 4; Medium-size Humanoid (zeetvah); HD 4d10+4; hp 23; Init +1 (Dex); Spd 30 ft.; AC 15 (+4 scale mail, +1 Dex); Melee +6 Longsword (1d8+1/crit 19-20 x2) or Ranged +5 Revolver (1d10/crit x3/Rng 100 ft.); SQ: Superior hearing, superior sense of smell; AL: N; SV Fort +5, Ref +2, Will +1; Str 12, Dex 13, Con 12, Int 14, Wis 10, Cha 12.

Skills and Feats: Bluff +3, Climb +3, Intimidate +2, Jump +2, Profession (Gagglezoomer Driver) +4, Sense Motive +2, Spot +1, Wilderness Lore +1; Dodge, Fortune's Fool, Mobility, Rapid Shot, Weapon Focus (Longsword).

Possessions: Scale Mail, Longsword, Backpack of Holding (see New Magical Items, Chapter Two), Revolver, Treasure (uncounted or sorted, stored in the backpack).

Notes: At the end of the Quest for the Throne storyline, Snarf is out of bullets in his revolver, but Aveeare has promised to help him replenish their supply.

History: A rural zeetvah of humble origins, Snarf was born into an average farming family. Liked by most, Snarf's biggest fault (in the eyes of his fellow zeetvah) was his tendency to daydream instead of working. He purchased a sword and began practicing fighting imaginary enemies. When he learned that the king was dead and a new quest for the throne was announced, Snarf thought a year of adventuring could give him a life on "easy street." Snarf set out on the road... not realizing his life had truly begun.

Snarf started small, stealing a gem from a passing orc's helmet, then went on to complete more noble missions. He recovered Etheah of the Woodland's wand of wishing, defeated the evil wizard Suthaze (twice), drove off a fearsome red dragon, liberated the city of Quessa, mastered the art of driving a gagglezoomer, survived the hazards of the Perpetual Pit, tamed a dark shade death leech, slew a dreaded mountain giant, killed the evil wizard Gathgor, won the heart of a beautiful warrior maiden, and rescued Zeetville from the terror of another red dragon... or so the tales go. Snarf was awarded the kingship of the valley and all zeetvahs, though now the crown sits upon a troubled brow. Snarf is getting bored.

I think Snarf represents the average guy. He is not super human, he is not super anything. He has a lot of luck, both good and bad. He has an outgoing personality, and talks his way in and out of a lot of trouble.

He loves women and especially loves Telerie. Their relationship is not touched on much in the strip. She fell for him because she thought he was so brave, but what she didn't know he was simply knocked crazy at the time. I think Snarf sort of grew on her and somewhere in their travels she fell in love with him. Snarf really can't remember their meeting and why she liked him. Of course Snarf loved her, she was beautiful and for some reason she seemed to like him, perhaps that is why he never pushed their relationship, he was and still is afraid she may leave him. Snarf would like to have a much closer relationship with her but he is basically too shy to speak what he feels. As the strip progressed, Telerie slowly took on the personality of my wife.

I always related to Snarf, he usually reacted the way I would in most of the critical situations. Actually some of the funny events that happened to Snarf, actually came from my real life. I looked at the strip as an exaggerated example of real life. We set some goals and work hard to achieve them. It is never easy, and unexpected things always happen on our way. We deal with adversity, try to overcome it, sometimes we can only "ride out" some of life's extreme events. Of course, the last most basic reaction, occasionally we just run away!!! The one thing I liked about Snarf, is that he hardly ever gave up and was always up for a good adventure.

Personality: Snarf's personality has changed since the beginning of his career. Originally out only for himself, wealth, and power, he has learned the value of friendship, courage, and found reward in helping others. He has also learned that life on the road suits him, and he prefers adventuring to "sitting around, getting fat." The heavy responsibility of kingship doesn't sit well with him, either. Snarf is in love with Telerie, though he is terrified to express his feelings. He hopes that eventually he'll be able to work up the courage to tell her just how he feels. Snarf is still a bit greedy and can be quick to anger, but he is also underestimated by most of his enemies, who do not understand how clever Snarf can be, how he has surrounded himself with valuable allies, and how luck usually goes his way when things are desperate.

SUTHAZE

Old Male Human

Wiz 12: CR 12; Medium-size Humanoid (human); HD 12d4; hp 30; Init +0; Spd 30 ft.; AC 10; SA Spells; AL: LE; SV Fort +5, Ref +4, Will +8; Str 12, Dex 11, Con 12, Int 17, Wis 11, Cha 10.

Skills and Feats: Alchemy +11, Bluff +6, Climb +1, Concentration +13, Escape Artist +2, Hide +3, Intimidate +6, Jump +1, Knowledge (Arcana) +15, Listen +0, Move Silently +0, Scry +11, Search +5, Spellcraft +15, Spot +2; Brew Potion, Combat Casting, Craft Rod, Craft Staff, Craft Wondrous Item, Maximize Spell, Quicken Spell, Scribe Scroll, Spell Mastery (Read Magic), Spell Penetration.

Spells Known: Wizard (4 / 5 / 5 / 5 / 3 / 3 / 2)

- 0- Arcane Mark, Dancing Lights, Detect Magic, Flare, Ghost Sound, Light, Mage Hand, Mending, Open/Close, Prestidigitation, Ray of Frost, Read Magic, Resistance
- 1- Burning Hands, Change Self, Charm Person, Mage Armor, Magic Missile, Ray of Enfeeblement, Shield, Sleep, Spider Climb
- 2- Alter Self, Endurance, Knock, Melf's Acid Arrow, Locate Object, Mirror Image, Pyrotechnics, Scare, Shatter
- 3- Clairaudience/Clairvoyance, Dispel Magic, Fireball, Flame Arrow, Haste, Lightning Bolt, Major Image, Mutate*, Suggestion
- 4- Arcane Eye, Charm Monster, Dimension Door, Locate Creature, Minor Creation, Polymorph Other, Scrying
- 5- Cone of Cold, Identity Crisis*, Seeming, Teleport
- 6- Chain Lightning, Mass suggestion, Mislead.

History: The "Tower of Suthaze" was on the map during the time of Snarf's grandparents. (Suthaze has been acquiring youthening magic to stave off truly old age.) For generations, Suthaze has hatched and launched evil schemes in his tower, quickly thwarting any-

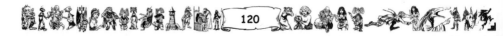

one who might rise to threaten him. He didn't always kill intruders, but he would always punish them, sometimes with his mutate spell (such as the case of Prince Raffendorf). His most prized acquisition ever was a powerful artifact, the hourglass of time-jumping. Suthaze began making regular trips into the future, picking up futuristic costumes, technology, and joined a motorcycle gang. When Suthaze's apprentice, Geezel, destroyed the hourglass of time-jumping and stole the "revolver" weapon, Suthaze led his magically-enslaved guards in hot pursuit. Through magical scrying, he saw Geezel had joined forces with two intruders—a zeetvah named Snarf and that rat prince, Raffendorf. During the struggle that followed, Snarf completely destroyed Suthaze's tower in a series of spectacular explosions, then shot Suthaze in the foot. Soon afterward, he took the dragon Willie to Quessa and terrified the populace into submission. Just when things were starting to look up for Suthaze, Snarf came charging in, driving a gagglezoomer straight into Suthaze. But you can't keep an evil wizard down. Escaping the Quessan prison was no problem, but now he's wandering the lands, looking for ways to amass the power to smite Snarf.

Personality: Suthaze does not like to be alone, which may seem strange for an old, evil wizard, but it's true. He likes having people to talk to, someone who will be waiting when he returns from jumps in time. He used to have grandiose evil schemes, but he's left those behind for now. Revenge is his focus—revenge against Snarf! (Still, he'd love to find some allies who would help meet his love of technology and desire for payback.)

TELERIE WINDYARM

Adult Female Human

Ftr 5, Bbn 1: CR 6; Medium-size Humanoid (human); HD 5d10+1d12+6; hp 63; Init +3 (+3 Dex); Spd 40 ft.; AC 15 (+4 chain shirt, +1 Dex); Melee +12/+7 Windsplitting Sword (1d8+7/crit 19-20 x3); SA: Rage 1/day; AL: CG; SV Fort +7, Ref +4, Will +2; Str 16, Dex 16, Con 13, Int 12, Wis 12, Cha 14.

Skills and Feats: Balance +4, Bluff +4, Climb +7, Heal +3, Intimidate +3, Jump +7, Ride +5, Search +3, Spot +4, Swim +5, Wilderness Lore +4; Armor Proficiency (Heavy), Armor Proficiency (Light), Armor Proficiency (Medium), Cleave, Combat Reflexes, Improved Bull Rush, Improved Unarmed Strike, Martial Weapon Proficiency, Power Attack, Shield Proficiency, Simple Weapon Proficiency, Weapon Focus (longsword), Weapon Specialization (longsword).

Possessions: Chain Shirt, Dagger, Windsplitting Sword (see New Magical Items, Chapter Two).

History: Telerie was raised as the daughter of the noble Lord Windyarm. She adored her warrior father, who fought with the family heirloom, the Windsplitting Sword. Her childhood was shattered when an evil wizard named Gathgor crippled her father and stole the family's fortune. From that day forward, Telerie

trained as a warrior, dreaming of revenge in the name Windyarm. But she was near to giving up when she saw a small zeetvah slay a mountain giant by himself. Convinced this warrior was just the ally she needed, she tricked the zeetvah and his companions to join her. Snarf helped her destroy Gathgor, and they have been friends since that day. When they returned to Zeetville, Telerie became fearful that Snarf would be killed by a red dragon and confessed to Snarf that she "lo-liked him...a lot." Snarf bravely defeated the dragon, and it dawned on Telerie that she would go anywhere with Snarf.

Personality: Telerie is courageous and dedicated, though she has a hot temper when roused. She admires bravery and resourcefulness in others, and is remarkably free of most racial prejudice. Telerie also lacks any sense of modesty, baring her body in front of friends without a hint of shame. She is in love with Snarf, but is afraid to tell him her true feelings. Until she works up the courage to make "a move" on the zeetvah, she hopes to continue adventuring with him.

"WILLIE" (Kizarvexius the Red)

Red Dragon - Young Adult Male

CR 12; Huge Dragon (fire); HD 19d12+95; hp 218; Init +4 (Improved Initiative); Spd 40 ft., fly 150 ft. (poor); AC 26 (-2 size, +18 natural); Melee Bite +27 (2d8+10), 2 claws +22 (2d6+5), 2 wings +22 (1d8+5), Tail Slap +22 (2d6+15), Crush (2d8+15); SA Breath Weapon, Fear; SQ Dmg Reduction 5/+1, Blindsight, Keen Senses, Immunities: Sleep, paralysis and other by type.; SV Fort +16, Ref +11, Wil +10; Str 31, Dex 10, Con 21, Int 6 (14), Wis 5 (15), Cha 14.

Skills and Feats: Bluff +4, Concentration +4, Knowledge (Duck) +2, Listen +3, Search +4, Spot +3; Improved Initiative.

Breath Weapon (Su): Willie can breathe a cone of fire. Though he is physically capable of using his breath weapon, he does not believe that a duck like himself can spit fire. Only when persuaded that he (as a duck) has been given some sort of special magical item or power (such as when Sneeve had him swallow the "magic" rock) will he be able to breathe fire—something that requires a Concentration check (DC 15) to accomplish.

Fire Subtype (Ex): Fire immunity, double damage from cold except on a successful save. Notes: If Willie ever comes to his senses and realizes his true nature (as Kizarvexius the red dragon), his stats revert to the numbers in parentheses. He also gains all typical skills and feats of a dragon of his age category, as well as spell-like abilities.

"One night der wuz a real bad storm an' da dragon got struck by lightning right in da head… we heard him thumping around outside da main tower… When we found him, he didn't even know who or what he was. So ol' Suthaze threw a spell on da dragon an' made him think he was a duck."

– Geezel

History: Suthaze's spell (see Identity Crisis, Chapter Three) worked, and the once-fierce red dragon became harmless—though the creature was still an effective deterrent to would-be thieves. Snarf freed Kizarvexius from the curse of the duck, after relieving Suthaze's treasury of magic wands. The dragon proceeded to kill most of Suthaze's guards and was hoarding the wizard's treasure for itself, when a series of explosions leveled Suthaze's tower. The boggled, wounded dragon collapsed—now permanently convinced it was a duck.

Suthaze was desperate to regain fortune and power, and realized that the mentally handicapped dragon was an easy ticket to both. He took Willie to Quessa, using the threat of the "dragon's" wrath if the king and his people did not obey. Willie never even saw Suthaze's second defeat by Snarf, and followed eagerly the zeetvah's suggestion to play a "game." After pretending to be defeated by Snarf and Aveeare, Willie attempted to fly south for the winter (like all good ducks).

It wasn't long before poor Willie realized he didn't know which way was south. Lost, confused, and frightened, he landed in the hills only a day's walk outside of Zeetville. Less than a day later, Newfert and Sneeve stumbled upon the sobbing dragon, and quickly grasped that a dragon that lisps, cries, and quacks was no threat. It was not difficult to talk the lonely dragon into returning with them to Zeetville, again "pretending" to be a real dragon. Snarf returned in time to challenge Newfert's claim to the throne, and the resulting hijinks caused Willie to burn Snarf (only first-degree) shortly before Snarf was crowned king of Zeetville.

Snarf has had his subjects lure Willie out of the valley with fish, but the confused dragon keeps coming back—since the zeetvahs are the nicest folk he has met (and they are good at catching fish).

Personality: The original Kizarvexius the red dragon is malevolent, evil, and intelligent—though the combination of magic and brain damage have left the poor wyrm forever convinced it is a mallard. Willie is actually quite likeable, and even the more villainous characters in the story don't treat him harshly. (It's just not right to see a dragon cry, something Willie does when scolded.) The duck/dragon speaks with a noticeable lisp ("Duckths love to thwim in the water!") and its forked tongue usually hangs out of the side of his mouth.

Willie never enters into combat willingly, running from anything that would pose a threat to an ordinary duck. It will cower when threatened, quickly breaking into tears and begging for mercy. If possible, it will fly away from danger in the manner of an unashamed coward. If cornered, however, Willie will fight with desperation and fury—likely shredding its would-be attackers to bloody bits. Willie feels terribly lonely, never understanding why other ducks fly away from every pond and lake it lands in. This loneliness (combined with it poor judgment of character) leads Willie to keep company with anyone who will put up with him, even evil wizards or scheming zeetvahs.

THE MAIN REASON I HAVE CONTINUED SNARFQUEST™ IS BECAUSE OF YOU, THE READERS. I'VE RECEIVED SO MANY GREAT LETTERS (AND A FEW BAD ONES) OVER THE PAST 6 YEARS. I TRULY THANK EACH AND EVERYONE OF YOU THAT HAVE WRITTEN ME OR ENJOYED READING THIS STRIP. I'M SORRY THAT I HAVEN'T HAD THE TIME TO ANSWER ALL OF YOUR LETTERS. WHO KNOWS, MAYBE SOMEDAY WE WILL BRING BACK "SNARFQUEST II" OR "SON OF SNARF", OR "SNARF THE 13TH"...

I'VE GOT SOME QUESTIONS TO ASK DIS GUY... HEY! IT'S WIERD OUT HERE! EVERYTHING IS WHITE, ALL WHITE.... GAAAA.

JUS' HOLD ON SNARF, YOU'RE NOT GOIN' OUT THERE WITHOUT ME, I COMIN' OUT WITH YA!

I DON'T UNDERSTAND ANY OF THIS... IT'S ALL STRANGE, LIKE ANOTHER DIMENSION!

I'M NOT GOIN' OUT DERE!

OH NO! DIS BE CRAZY.!!

... OR PERHAPS, "NIGHTMARE ON SNARF ST.", HOW 'BOUT, "SNARF WARS, THE RETURN OF THE ZEETVAH", "SNARF WARS, SUTHAZE STRIKES BACK", OR "SNARF TREK, THE SEARCH FOR SNARF"...

WHAT'S ALL OF DIS "SNARF @*☆#"?

OR "ZEETVAH, MUTANT NINJA SNARF-ER"... NO, NO, I GOT IT... "SNARF'S EXCELLENT ADVENTURE!!

OH MY, GEEZEL, IT'S REALLY STRANGE OUT HERE... WATCH YOUR STEP.

ME SURE DON'T KNOW WHY ME BE GOIN' OUT HERE!

I'VE GOT TO INVESTIGATE THIS NEW DIMENSION. HOW DID I MISS THIS? B.B., KEEP EVERYONE BACK INSIDE, OKAY?

SURE.

YOU GUYS BE CAREFUL.

HEY! WHAT ARE YOU GUYS DOIN' OUT HERE? GET BACK IN THAT PANEL, RIGHT NOW! HURRY! EVERYTHING WILL DISAPPEAR IN A SECOND!

YOU JUS' HOLD ON, DUDE! YOU'RE GONNA ANSWER SOME QUESTIONS...

HURRY GEEZEL.... C'MON SNARF, LET'S GET BACK IN THE PANEL.

LOOK! DERE BE A B'JILLION PEOPLE OUT DERE!

HOLY COW!

C'MON YOU GUYS! DIS PANEL THING IS GETTIN' SMALLER!

WHAT'S DAT?

WHAT IS HAPPENING?

POOF

END!?!

A couple of years ago I was reading the complete SnarfQuest strip that ran in Dragon Magazine, and it hit me all of a sudden that I had illustrated my own life. I hadn't realized it at the time I was doing the strip. The SnarfQuest strip ran for almost 9 years in Dragon Magazine. The strip started the first year I went to work at TSR. My career was just beginning and I felt I was on the threshold of a great adventure, and I was. Just like Snarf, I had left my own small town in Kentucky with my wife and two little children and went all the way to Wisconsin to seek fortune and fame. My motivation, at that time, was to "make it", become a famous artist, make lots of money, and come back to my little town as "somebody"! I was Snarf. I noticed that as the strip continued, Snarf began to mellow.

He still had his goal in mind but he started to enjoy the journey even more. When he finally became king, his whole attitude had changed. It wasn't what he thought it would be. There wasn't a quitting point. It was just more work and a lot more responsibilities, and getting there was a lot more fun.

Nothing is what you think it is in your dreams. I had become a successful artist and was supporting my family quite well, but it took a lot of work, many battles, a lot of luck and a never-give-up attitude, which I think Snarf has. In my most current strip, Snarf gave up his crown and went back to adventuring. As with life, the crowns that we pursue are not what counts, it is the friends, and the adventures along the journey that mean the most. My adventures are my next painting or project. Just trying to get better at my skills and have a lot of fun on the way.

A word from Larry Elmore, creator of *SnarfQuest*

OPEN GAME LICENSE Version 1.0a

The following text is the property of Wizards of the Coast, Inc. and is Copyright 2000 Wizards of the Coast, Inc ("Wizards"). All Rights Reserved.

1. Definitions: (a)"Contributors" means the copyright and/or trademark owners who have contributed Open Game Content; (b)"Derivative Material" means copyrighted material including derivative works and translations (including into other computer languages), potation, modification, correction, addition, extension, upgrade, improvement, compilation, abridgment or other form in which an existing work may be recast, transformed or adapted; (c) "Distribute" means to reproduce, license, rent, lease, sell, broadcast, publicly display, transmit or otherwise distribute; (d)"Open Game Content" means the game mechanic and includes the methods, procedures, processes and routines to the extent such content does not embody the Product Identity and is an enhancement over the prior art and any additional content clearly identified as Open Game Content by the Contributor, and means any work covered by this License, including translations and derivative works under copyright law, but specifically excludes Product Identity. (e) "Product Identity" means product and product line names, logos and identifying marks including trade dress; artifacts; creatures characters; stories, storylines, plots, thematic elements, dialogue, incidents, language, artwork, symbols, designs, depictions, likenesses, formats, poses, concepts, themes and graphic, photographic and other visual or audio representations; names and descriptions of characters, spells, enchantments, personalities, teams, personas, likenesses and special abilities; places, locations, environments, creatures, equipment, magical or supernatural abilities or effects, logos, symbols, or graphic designs; and any other trademark or registered trademark clearly identified as Product identity by the owner of the Product Identity, and which specifically excludes the Open Game Content; (f) "Trademark" means the logos, names, mark, sign, motto, designs that are used by a Contributor to identify itself or its products or the associated products contributed to the Open Game License by the Contributor (g) "Use", "Used" or "Using" means to use, Distribute, copy, edit, format, modify, translate and otherwise create Derivative Material of Open Game Content. (h) "You" or "Your" means the licensee in terms of this agreement.

2. The License: This License applies to any Open Game Content that contains a notice indicating that the Open Game Content may only be Used under and in terms of this License. You must affix such a notice to any Open Game Content that you Use. No terms may be added to or subtracted from this License except as described by the License itself. No other terms or conditions may be applied to any Open Game Content distributed using this License.

3.Offer and Acceptance: By Using the Open Game Content You indicate Your acceptance of the terms of this License.

4. Grant and Consideration: In consideration for agreeing to use this License, the Contributors grant You a perpetual, worldwide, royalty-free, non-exclusive license with the exact terms of this License to Use, the Open Game Content.

5.Representation of Authority to Contribute: If You are contributing original material as Open Game Content, You represent that Your Contributions are Your original creation and/or You have sufficient rights to grant the rights conveyed by this License.

6.Notice of License Copyright: You must update the COPYRIGHT NOTICE portion of this License to include the exact text of the COPYRIGHT NOTICE of any Open Game Content You are copying, modifying or distributing, and You must add the title, the copyright date, and the copyright holder's name to the COPYRIGHT NOTICE of any original Open Game Content you Distribute.

7. Use of Product Identity: You agree not to Use any Product Identity, including as an indication as to compatibility, except as expressly licensed in another, independent Agreement with the owner of each element of that Product Identity. You agree not to indicate compatibility or co-adaptability with any Trademark or Registered Trademark in conjunction with a work containing Open Game Content except as expressly licensed in another, independent Agreement with the owner of such Trademark or Registered Trademark. The use of any Product Identity in Open Game Content does not constitute a challenge to the ownership of that Product Identity. The owner of any Product Identity used in Open Game Content shall retain all rights, title and interest in and to that Product Identity.

8. Identification: If you distribute Open Game Content You must clearly indicate which portions of the work that you are distributing are Open Game Content.

9. Updating the License: Wizards or its designated Agents may publish updated versions of this License. You may use any authorized version of this License to copy, modify and distribute any Open Game Content originally distributed under any version of this License.

10 Copy of this License: You MUST include a copy of this License with every copy of the Open Game Content You Distribute.

11. Use of Contributor Credits: You may not market or advertise the Open Game Content using the name of any Contributor unless You have written permission from the Contributor to do so.

12 Inability to Comply: If it is impossible for You to comply with any of the terms of this License with respect to some or all of the Open Game Content due to statute, judicial order, or governmental regulation then You may not Use any Open Game Material so affected.

13 Termination: This License will terminate automatically if You fail to comply with all terms herein and fail to cure such breach within 30 days of becoming aware of the breach. All sublicenses shall survive the termination of this License.

14 Reformation: If any provision of this License is held to be unenforceable, such provision shall be reformed only to the extent necessary to make it enforceable.

15. COPYRIGHT NOTICE

Open Game License v 1.0a Copyright 2000, Wizards of the Coast, Inc.
System Reference Document Copyright 2000, Wizards of the Coast, Inc.; Authors Jonathan Tweet, Monte Cook, Skip Williams, based on original material by E. Gary Gygax and Dave Arneson.
Sovereign Stone Campaign Sourcebook Copyright 2001, Sovereign Press, Inc.; Authors Timothy Kidwell, Jamie Chambers, Don Perrin, based on original material by Larry Elmore, Margaret Weis, and Tracy Hickman.
SnarfQuest RPG World Book Copyright 2002, Elmore Productions, Inc; Authors Larry Elmore and Jamie Chambers, based on original material by Larry Elmore.